Designs for Needlepoint and Latch Hook Rugs

By Dorothy Kaestner

Four Way Bargello
Needlepoint Bargello
Designs for Needlepoint and Latch Hook Rugs

Designs for Needlepoint and Latch Hook Rugs

Dorothy Kaestner

Photographs by George F. Kaestner

Charles Scribner's Sons   New York

Library of Congress Cataloging in Publication Data

Kaestner, Dorothy.
    Designs for needlepoint and latch hook rugs.

    Bibliography: p. 177
    1. Rugs.   2. Canvas embroidery—Patterns.
I. Title.
TT850.K3   746.7′4   76-50111
ISBN 0-684-14837-4

1 3 5 7 9 11 13 15 17 19 M/C 20 18 16 14 12 10 8 6 4 2

Printed in the United States of America

To my mother, who enjoyed hooking rugs and inspired me to work with my hands and my mind

ACKNOWLEDGMENTS

Many thanks first of all to Elinor Parker for suggesting this book. My gratitude to Ms. Mary Ryan and Mr. Richard Bartlett of the Victoria and Albert Museum in London who were so courteous to me, also Mr. A. C. Elwick and Mr. E. P. Larche of Liberty's of London for their generosity in allowing me the privilege of reproducing any of the rugs in their department, and to Bucilla for their latch hook directions.
To all my helpers in stitching on some of the rugs: Mrs. George Park, Mrs. Joan de Selding, Mrs. Cindy Seigler Brown, Mrs. Lucy Rowan, Mrs. Joan Keever, Nancy Love, Anne Tomasello, Amy Fink, and George, who also blocked and finished them. Thanks also to Mrs. L. J. Schettino and Mrs. F. Douglas Adams, Jr.

Foreword

I can first remember my mother hooking rugs when I was a child of about eight or ten. Dad would make a frame by putting four narrow boards together with C clamps. She would balance this on the backs of four straight chairs. All our old worn-out clothes would be cut up and she either would use the color as it was or sometimes would bleach and redye the clothes to get the colors she needed.

Mother was not an artist, so her designs were very simple. She used burlap bags for her base fabric; they were a bit sturdier then.

In later years, when the latch hook method of hooking became available, she switched to that method. It does not require a frame; just a card table is all that is needed.

Contents

Acknowledgments *vii*

Foreword *ix*

Introduction *1*

General Working Instructions *3*

The Patterns

   Blanche's Blocks   *9*

   Dottie's Blocks   *14*

   Small Solid-Color Blocks   *17*

   Octagon Rug   *18*

   Red and Green Hexagon Design   *23*

   Iranian Multiblock Rug   *30*

   Patchwork Medallion—Liberty's   *40*

   Caucasian (Kuba) Nineteenth Century   *58*

   Pink Samarkand   *64*

   Gold Bukhara   *78*

   Red Bukhara   *86*

   Gold and Off-White "Alhambra Door"   *92*

   Bright Green and Teal Moorish Design   *98*

   Early Seventeenth-Century Isfahan   *104*

   Red and Gold Swasti   *120*

   Blue-Green Bargello Rug   *126*

   Stair Risers and Treads   *134*

   Dragon   *150*

   Three Giraffes   *154*

   Odds and Ends   *169*

   Snowflake Latch Hook   *171*

   Doll-House Rugs:

      Red and Gold Persian   *172*

      Adaptation of a Hooked Rug Design   *175*

Canvas Sizes   *176*

Bibliography   *177*

xi

Designs for Needlepoint and Latch Hook Rugs

Introduction

When my second book, *Needlepoint Bargello*, was just about completed, my editor, Elinor Parker, asked me if I would work on a book about handmade rugs. Since I already had a rug in progress and others in mind I agreed to take on the challenge.

The first thing I did was to go downstairs from her office to the Scribner Book Store and purchase five books on Oriental rugs. I've had many hours of enjoyment poring over them since. At another time I went to the Metropolitan Museum book store and purchased another five books. From this collection of books I studied the colors used in the antique rugs, especially those that were dyed with the natural dyes of antiquity. I also studied the types of motifs that were used, which were many. Most of them had a pattern throughout the rug plus several borders. My idea was to simplify some of the motifs and borders and present them so that today's needle-worker can use them in various ways, not necessarily copying them verbatim. Some are charted almost like the original, while others have been changed quite a bit.

In May of 1974 George and I took a trip to London to photograph some of the beautiful old rugs in the Victoria and Albert Museum. I had written ahead to ask permission and explained my reason. The staff at the museum were most accommodating. Ms. Mary Ryan of public relations assured me that I could reproduce any of the rugs that I wished. Mr. Richard Bartlett unlocked the enclosures of the rugs, turned off the burglar alarms, turned on the lights, gave us a catalog of the rugs, and left us to photograph any or all. We spent two days there.

Another day, while walking up Regent Street, we noticed some beautiful Persian rugs in the window of Liberty's of London. We went in and visited the rug department. We introduced ourselves to Mr. A. C. Elwick, their carpet buyer, and explained why we were in London. He very graciously offered us the privilege of photographing and reproducing any of the rugs there. He and Mr. E. P. Larche, the outside

1

representative for Oriental rugs, spent some time with us explaining where some of the rugs came from, some of the present-day techniques of giving new rugs the patina that older rugs have, how colors have been altered by bleaching, and so on. George and I are very grateful to these people, who were so kind and cordial to us.

Most needleworkers today have become used to the even dyeing of yarns and bemoan any slight variation of color. The yarns that were naturally dyed years ago for making Oriental rugs were done so quite unevenly and this showed up in the weaving of the rugs. Some of the variation in color was extremely pronounced and made stripes across the rugs, which is called an "abrash." This showed up mostly in those that had a larger ground area. It wasn't possible to dye in large enough quantities to have one dye lot for an entire rug. The nomads of antiquity had to contend with different water supplies where the mineral content varied and this made the colors vary.

I did some home dyeing with natural dyes such as logwood, brazilwood, fustic, madder, cochineal, marigolds, goldenrod, indigo, osage orange, barberry, onion skins, and so forth, trying to achieve the colors used in the ancient rugs. I succeeded in getting some of the lovely colors but was not able to get the bright turkey red that was obtained from madder. Some of the mordants used for this color I would not use in my kitchen and others were kept secret. However, I did get some beautiful reds and pinks with the madder and with the cochineal; also with a combination of the two. I have not given any dye formulas. There are many dye books available for any of you who would like to try it; see the Bibliography.

I have worked samples of some rug patterns using the natural-dye yarns to show the lovely effect they give. Where there was a sizable ground, I worked in the continental stitch so the striping of color would go straight across the piece rather than on the diagonal. Some of these samples were done on #18 canvas with a single strand of yarn so that I wouldn't have yards of swatches.

For some of the designs there is a completed rug along with small samples of other color combinations. There are some suggestions of how to do a given rug in another stitch or technique.

Some of the designs I originated at my shop; not all are taken from old examples. The designs also vary from simple to complex and from small to large. Many can be made larger or smaller; borders can be interchanged to create your own rug. Most are charted, while others are line drawings.

PLATE 1   Blanche's Blocks 1, pages 8–13

PLATE 2   Blanche's Blocks 2, pages 8–13

PLATE 3   Dottie's Blocks, pages 14–15

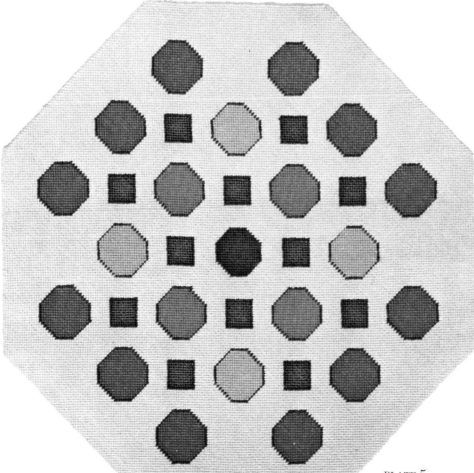

PLATE 5
Octagon Rug, pages 18-22

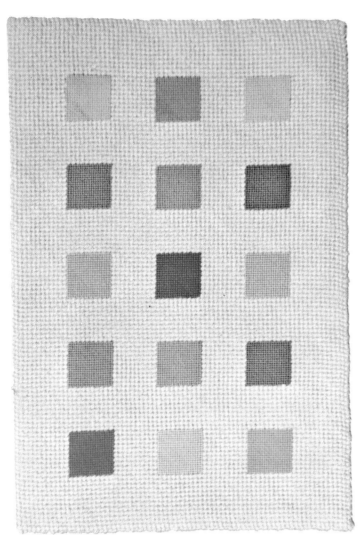

PLATE 4

Small Solid-Color Blocks, pages 16–17

PLATE 6

Red and Green Hexagon Design, pages 23–29

PLATE 7
Iranian Multiblock Rug, pages 30–39

PLATE 8
Iranian Multiblock Rug,
pages 30–39

PLATE 9
Liberty Doll-House Rug,
pages 30–39, 172–173

PLATE 10
Patchwork Medallion Rug,
pages 40–57

PLATE 11   Caucasian (Kuba) Nineteenth-Century Rug, pages 58–63

PLATE 12

Pink Samarkand Rug,
pages 64–77

PLATE 13
Gold Bukhara Rug, pages 78–85

PLATE 14
Gold Bukhara,
two variations of borders

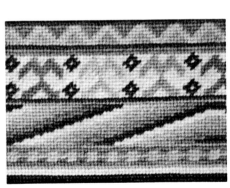

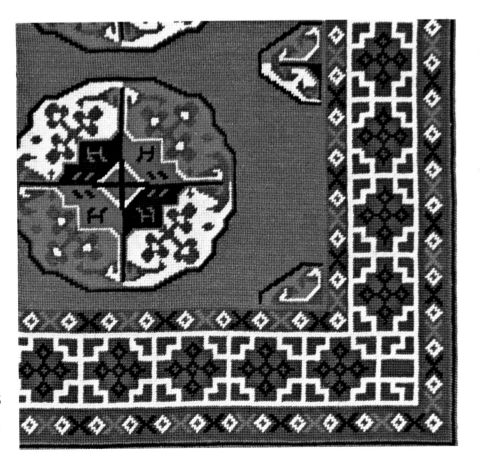

PLATE 15
Red Bukhara Rug,
pages 86–91

PLATE 16 **Gold and Off-White "Alhambra Door,"** pages 92–97

PLATE 17

Green border

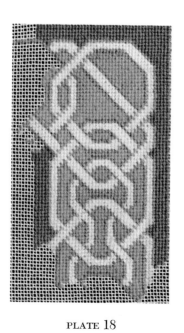

PLATE 18

Blue border

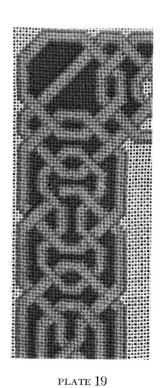

PLATE 19

Brick red border

PLATE 20   **Bright Green and Teal Moorish Design, pages 98–103**

PLATE 21

Early Seventeenth-Century Isfahan Rug,
pages 104–119

PLATE 22   Red and Gold Swasti Rug, pages 120–125

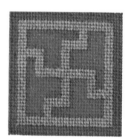

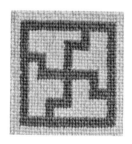

PLATE 23

Swasti Swatches

PLATE 24   Swasti Swatches

PLATE 25   Blue-Green Bargello Rug, pages 126–133

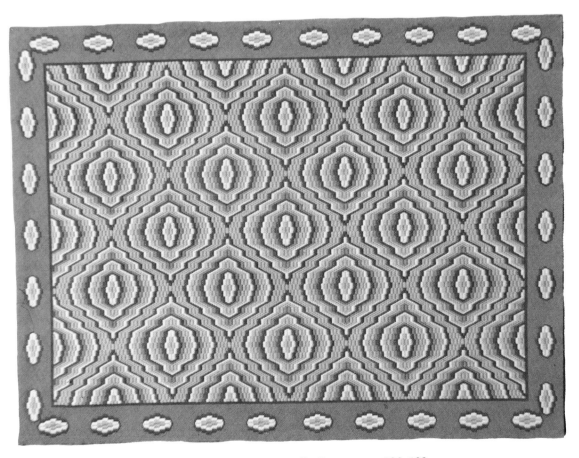

PLATE 26   Coral Bargello Rug, pages 126–133

PLATE 27   **Yellow-Gold Bargello Pillow, pages 126–133**

PLATE 29   **Dragon Rug, pages 150–153**

PLATE 28   Stair Risers and Treads, pages 134–149

PLATE 30   Three Giraffes Rug, pages 154–167

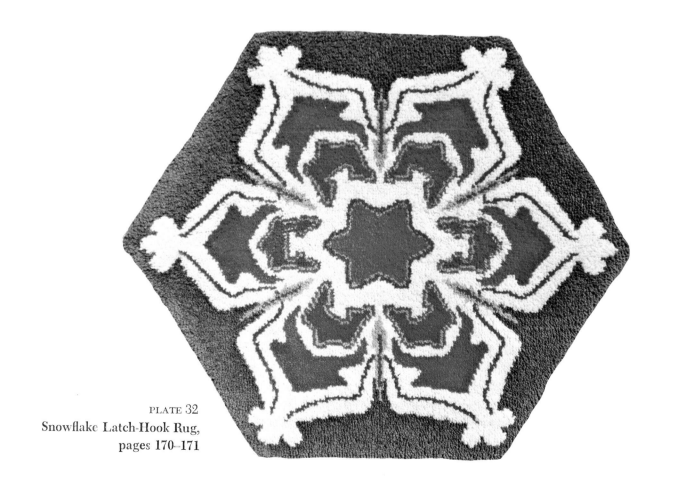

PLATE 32
Snowflake Latch-Hook Rug,
pages 170–171

PLATE 31   Odds and Ends Rug, pages 168–169

PLATE 33   Red and Gold Persian Doll-House Rug, pages 172–173

PLATE 34

Doll-House Rug,
pages 174–175

General Working Instructions

Stitches

Tent Stitch

Whenever tent stitch is referred to, use the basketweave method where possible. When there are single lines of stitches, you will have to work in continental stitch. If an unbroken line is desired in outlining, it can be worked in cross stitch, using two strands of yarn instead of three.

Basketweave Stitch, or Diagonal Tent Stitch

To work with the grain of the canvas, first place a stitch in the upper right corner of your canvas (assuming that you are working a square). Now examine the weave of the canvas. If the canvas threads that are to be covered next are vertical (shaded in left diagram), then your next stitch will be placed to the left of the corner stitch. If, on the other hand, the next row of stitching shows horizontal threads (shaded in second diagram), then your next stitch will be below the corner stitch.

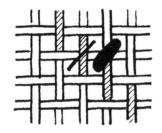 

In other words, you work from the top down when covering vertical canvas threads or from the bottom up when covering the horizontal canvas threads. The third diagram shows the progression of rows.

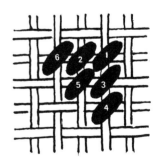

I have found that this method keeps your stitches more even. When worked in the opposite direction, one row looks a little different from the other. Try working a small area as described, then work a small area in the opposite manner and you will see the difference.

3

Continental Stitch

The continental stitch is worked from the right of the canvas toward the left of the canvas, or from the top of the canvas toward the bottom of the canvas. To work horizontally, place each stitch to the left of the previous stitch (first four stitches in diagram). To work vertically, place each stitch below the previous stitch (next four stitches in diagram). The remaining stitches in the diagram explain how to work a single line in various directions.

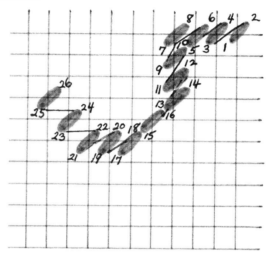

Bargello Stitch

This is a straight up-and-down stitch covering two or more threads of the canvas. The basic bargello is a stitch covering four threads and stepping up or down by two threads. This is referred to as a 4-2 step. The rug and pillow shown are a 4-2 step.

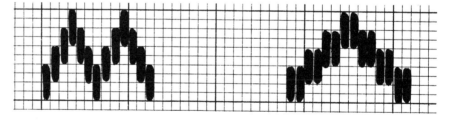

Long-Arm Cross Stitch

The long-arm cross stitch is worked over two horizontal threads. As shown in the diagram, come up at 1, go down at 2, come up at 3, go down at 4, come up at 5, go down at 6, come up at 7, go down at 8, and so on.

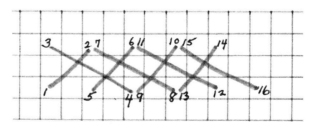

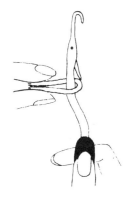

STEP 1 Fold a piece of yarn in half (ends even) and slip hook through loop so that latch is above and open.

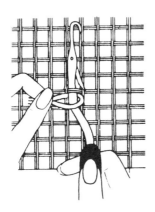

STEP 2 Starting at extreme lower left corner of printed design, with correct color, insert hook in one mesh and out the mesh directly above so that threads of canvas are over hook and latch is open.

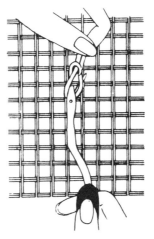

STEP 3 Move the left hand (holding ends of yarn) up and to the right so that you can catch the yarn in hook.

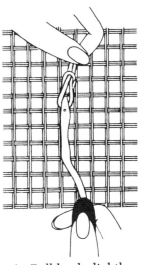

STEP 4 Pull hook slightly, closing latch over yarn. *Do not let go of the ends in fingers.*

Latch Hooking

Latch hook rugs are worked on a 3- to 4-mesh-to-the-inch canvas. Some meshes come in widths of 32″, 37″, 42″, and 64″.

Latch hooking should always be done in one direction, starting at one end and working each subsequent row above the one just finished. I find a card table best for holding the canvas. Bring the edge of the canvas toward you so that the working row bends over the edge of the table. This makes it easier to put the hook into the canvas. A covered brick makes a good weight to hold the canvas while you are hooking.

Work each row completely across the rug beginning at the extreme lower left (or lower right) and working to right (or left), hooking proper colors as charted.

After you have completed 10″ or 12″ of the rug it is helpful to start rolling the finished end of rug so that it will not be so cumbersome—fasten the roll at the ends with large safety pins.

The regular latch hook yarn comes in 1-ounce packages ready cut to a length of 2½″. There is a rya-type yarn, which is cut to a length of 4″. Use one piece of the regular yarn for each knot and three pieces of the rya for each knot. The rya yarn, of course, makes a higher pile. You can also use Persian yarn by cutting it yourself to whatever length you wish. Three of the three-strand pieces, or nine strands, are used. This gives a finer look to a latch rug.

On the latch canvas you can also work tent stitch, using quickpoint yarn.

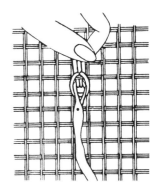

STEP 5 Pull hook down so that you are pulling it back through mesh, until ends of yarn over hook are visible, then let go of the ends in fingers and pull hook completely through, pulling ends of yarn through loop, forming the knot. If ends of yarn are even, pull them to tighten knot. *If they are not even, pull the shorter end so that they are even, thus tightening knot at the same time.*

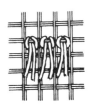

STEP 6 Shows three completed knots.

Courtesy of Bucilla

Canvas

Canvas is supposed to be an even-weave material. It is not always so. Also, the count of the mesh varies from roll to roll, as you will see by some of the measurements of patterns I list.

Sometimes we get a roll of #10 canvas and it might count to be 9 or 11 mesh to the inch. This makes a difference in the finished size of the pattern if you work from a chart. Some #12 and #14 canvases have come through at 12½ or 13 one way and 14 the other way. Your canvas dealer cannot help this; he has to take what the looms have produced. So whenever you have to stitch two pieces of canvas together, be sure to purchase all the canvas at the same time from the same roll. Also, be sure to work the two pieces in the same direction.

It is almost impossible to buy a roll of canvas today without knots or flaws. If one tried to cut canvas to avoid flaws there would be considerable waste.

It's very easy to repair a knotted canvas or one that you may have accidentally cut when cutting out stitches. Cut the knot out, then take a piece of the thread from the canvas at the edge. Put this thread through your needle and weave it in, copying the weave of the cut thread. The beginning and end of this new thread should overlap the cut part by 1 inch in each direction. When you start stitching, just work over the double threads as if they were one.

If you have other canvas that has a finer thread in the weave, you can use this. Then the double thread will be easier to work over.

Since canvas does vary in the number of mesh per inch, don't be afraid to purchase another ¼ or ⅓ yard extra for your rug when working from a chart. The amount of money spent is nothing compared to the irritation if, before you come to the end of your pattern, you have come to the end of your canvas.

Yarn Requirements and Needles

One cannot always estimate yarn requirements accurately. First of all, we use the yarn differently; one person may work more loosely than another or leave longer ends to be cut off. In general, however, ¼ pound of Persian yarn does about 144 square inches on 10-mesh canvas. That is a square of 12″ by 12″.

NEEDLE SIZE	CANVAS MESH	NUMBER OF STRANDS
18	10	3 or 4
20	12 to 14	2 or 3
14 or 16	5	9

TENT ST.	BARGELLO
3	4
2	3
9	

We have been able to get 10-, 12-, and 13-mesh canvas 54″ wide and 10-mesh 60″ wide.

To Transfer Drawings to Canvas

Use heavy tracing paper or drawing paper thin enough to see through. Don't cut it up into page-size pieces, but trace each page onto the paper in its proper place, using a black marking pen. Then tape your traced papers together to reconstruct the full-size pattern. Now place your canvas over this drawing, and, using a waterproof pen such as a Nepo or Sharpie, lightly trace the drawing onto your canvas. I repeat, use your pen lightly, do not make a heavy line. On delicate colors it may show through your stitching.

Rather than trying to work from many separate pages of a chart, have each page Xeroxed, then tape the pages together with magic transparent tape. Now you will have a complete chart from which to work and you will also be able to refer more easily to the colorplate.

It is helpful to color in some of a chart with colored pencils. Taping a small piece of the colored yarn to an area also helps.

An easy way to copy a design in the opposite direction is to hold a mirror behind the one you are copying.

If the drawing has been reduced in size you will need to have it enlarged. This can be done by tracing it on your tracing paper with a fine-line black marker and then taking it to a shop that makes photostats, which can enlarge the drawing to the size required. However, if you have a camera and a slide projector, you can photograph the drawing and project it onto a large sheet of paper taped to a wall or door. Then you can trace the projected drawing.

The Patterns

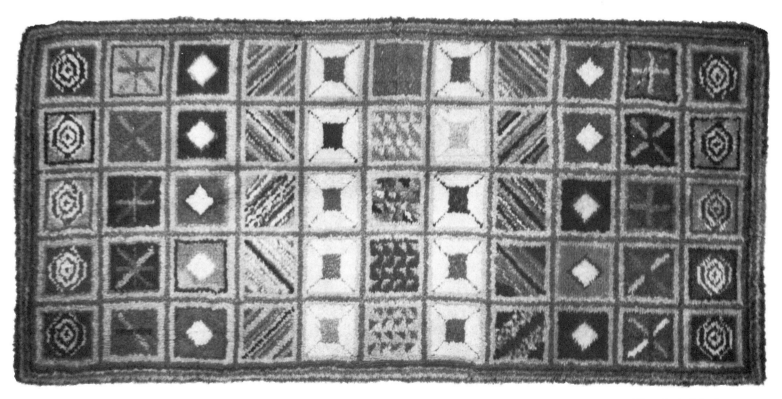

Blanche's Blocks 1

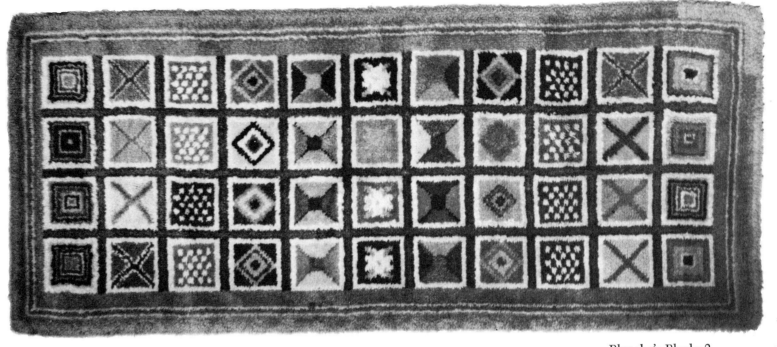

Blanche's Blocks
Mother's Latch Hook Rugs

These two rugs were designed and hooked by my mother, Mrs. Frederick Taylor, some years ago. (Colorplates 1 and 2.)

When the American Lady Rug Company discontinued business we had a stock of assorted colors of their rug yarn. We gave all of it to Mother along with some canvas.

I'm sure that she never bothered with graph paper to do her planning before hooking. She probably decided on the size of block to use, then worked out each row of designs as she went along. She used up small quantities of color by working stripes or even using one shade on one side of a design and another shade on the other side. This type of design is very simple to enlarge or reduce. Just add or take away blocks, increase or decrease the size of the blocks, or add more space between the blocks. The borders can also be wider and varied.

This principle of design adapts itself to needlepoint as well as latch hooking. Most of the designs that follow can be made by either method.

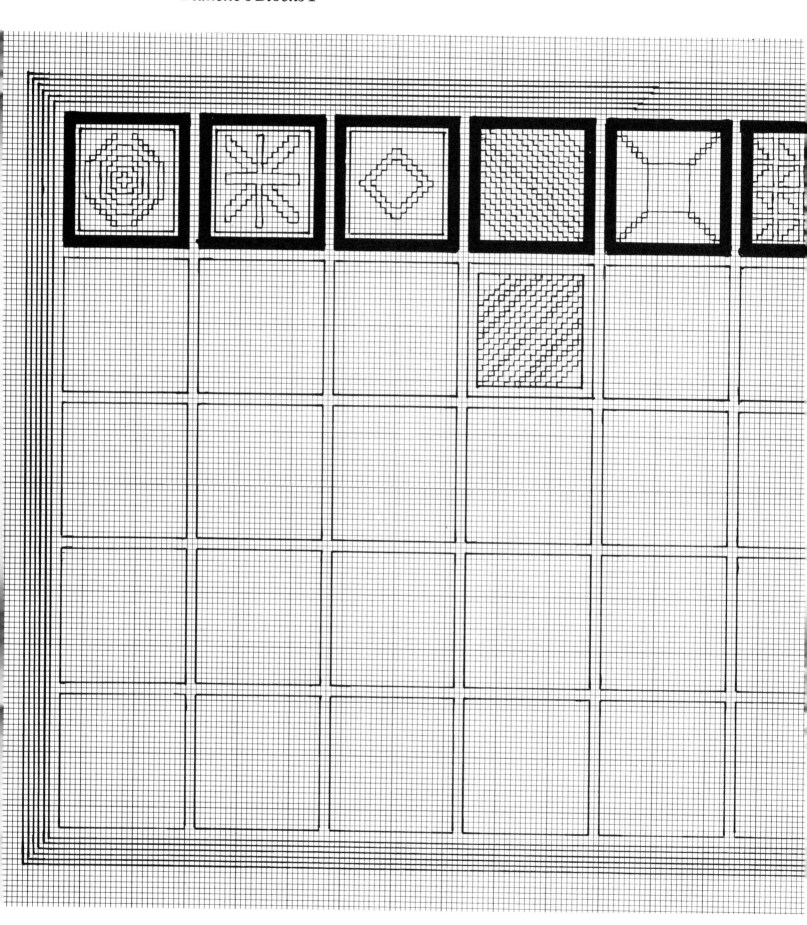

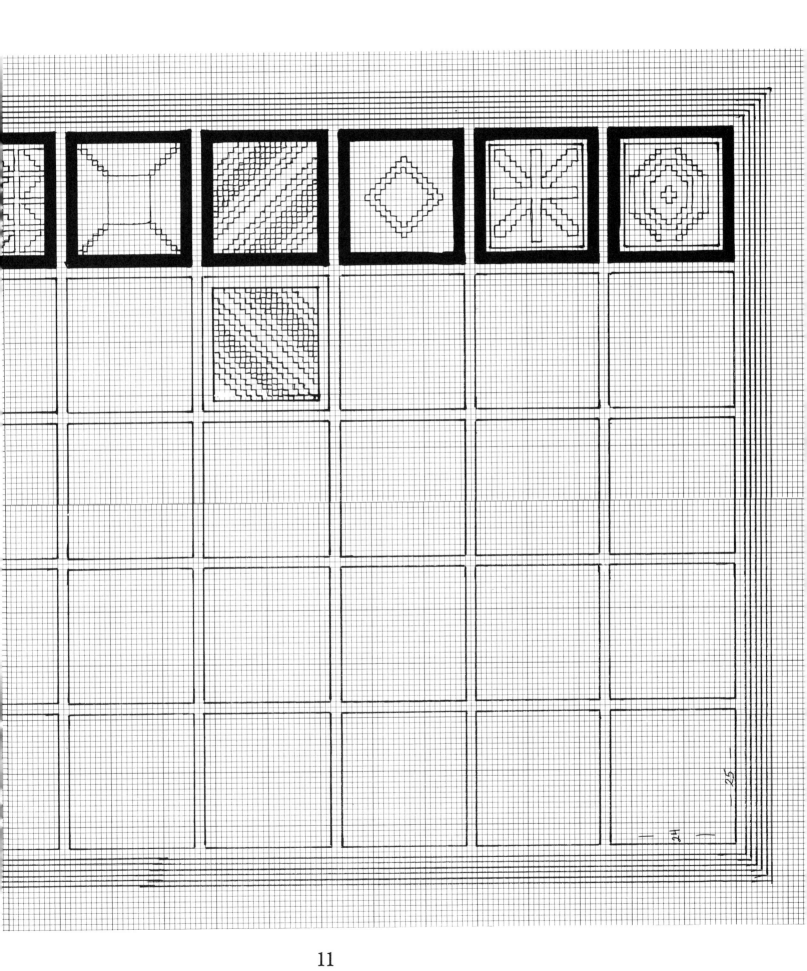

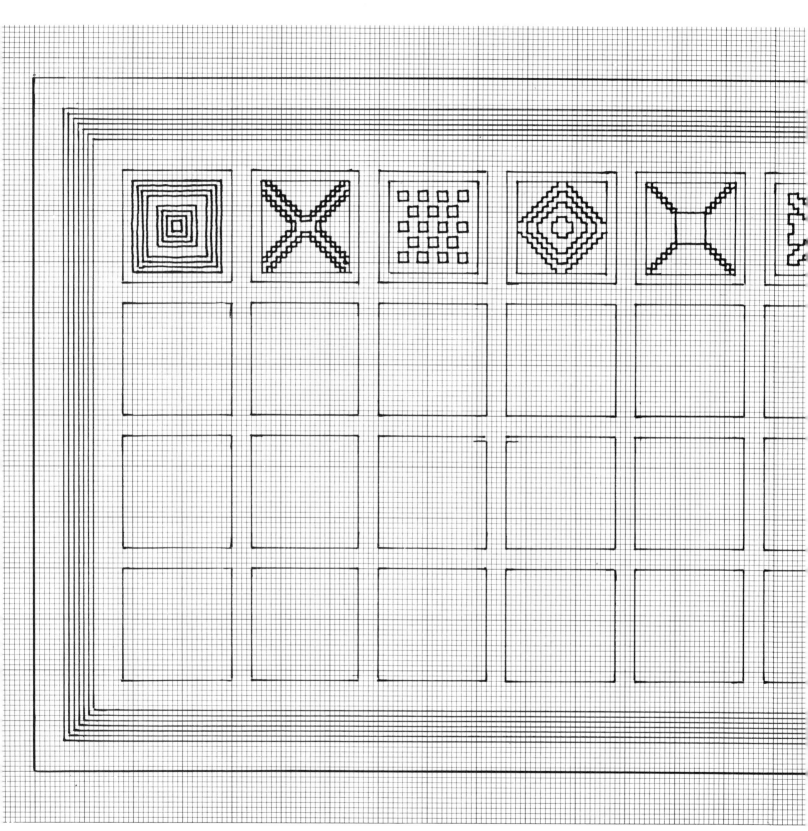

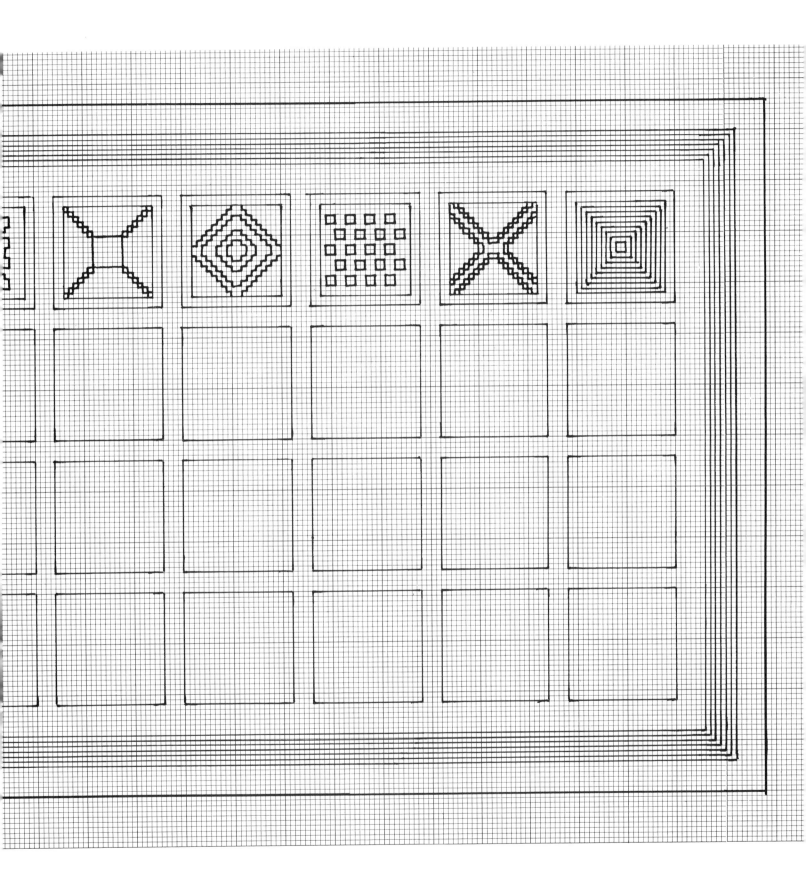

Dottie's Blocks

Here are three more simple block patterns for latch hook or
needlepoint which I designed. The first one shows how you can
repeat the blocks in a diagonal pattern instead of straight
across. You could use up small quantities of colors like a
patchwork quilt, or work out definite color schemes.

For the blue pillow design shown in plate 3, I separated the

blocks with two rows of medium blue, two rows of alternating light and medium blue, and another two rows of medium blue. I used four shades of blue and an off-white. It was worked on 12-mesh canvas, which was certainly not an even weave. Each small block measures 2″ by 2¼″ instead of 2″ square. The finished piece measures 12¼″ by 13¾″. The block scheme can be expanded to any length to make a rug.

The first four blocks across and the first five blocks down were used for the pillow.

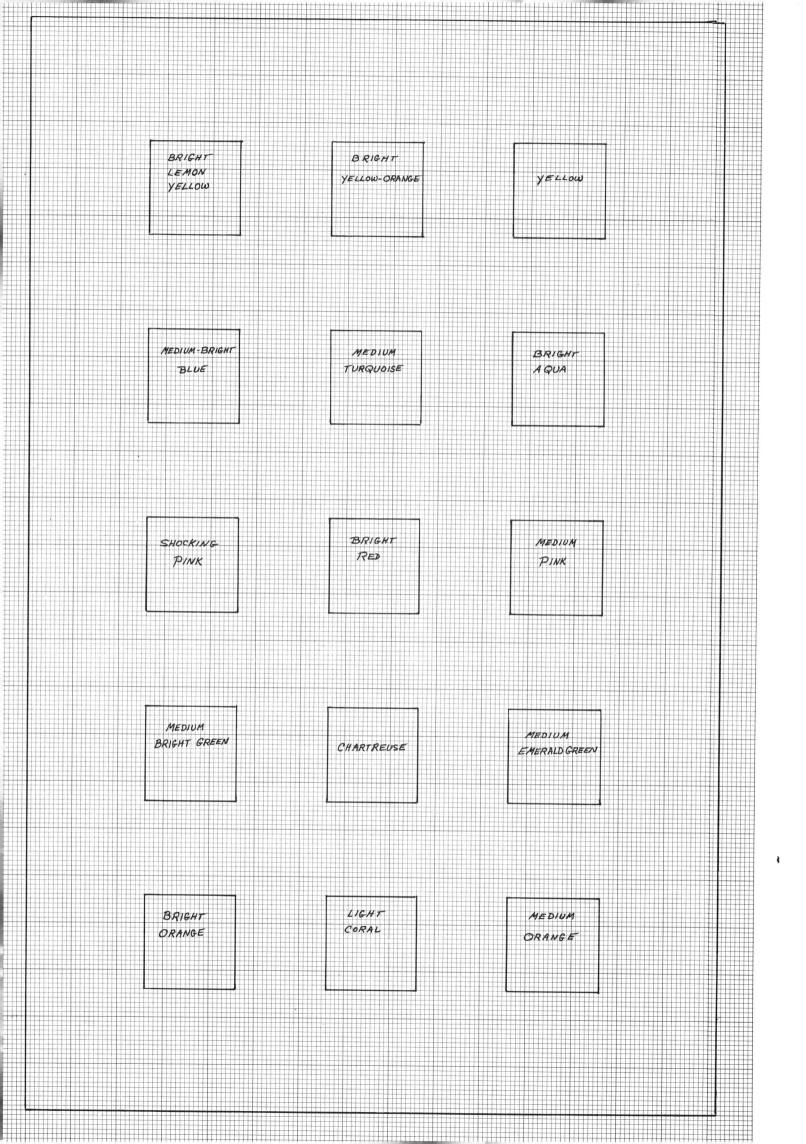

Small Solid-Color Blocks

As shown—15″ by 23″

The sample shown in plate 4 is just an example of what could be a rug of any size. This is another good way of using up leftover yarns. If the number of blocks was doubled in width and in length (six blocks by ten blocks), the rug would measure 27″ by 41″.

I used #5 penelope canvas so that I could use large and small stitches. The small blocks were stitched in every hole (10 stitches = 1″), while the background was stitched in the large holes only (5 stitches = 1″). This gives a slightly sculptured look. It could also be done in reverse by using the large stitch in the blocks and the small stitch for the background. The size of the blocks could be changed, for example, 3″ by 3″, 4″ by 4″, and so on.

The three-strand Persian yarn, as it comes, was used for the small stitch and three times that was used for the large stitch. It takes approximately five 33″ strands of yarn for each 2″ by 2″ block. The background of the small-size rug takes about 10 ounces. The larger rug would take about 40 ounces.

Certainly, any novice could tackle this design.

Octagon Rug

This is another block design in a different shape that would
be easy for the beginner. It was worked on 10-mesh canvas using
the three strands of Persian yarn. The worked sample measures
21″ across. The chart has two sizes shown; the larger one

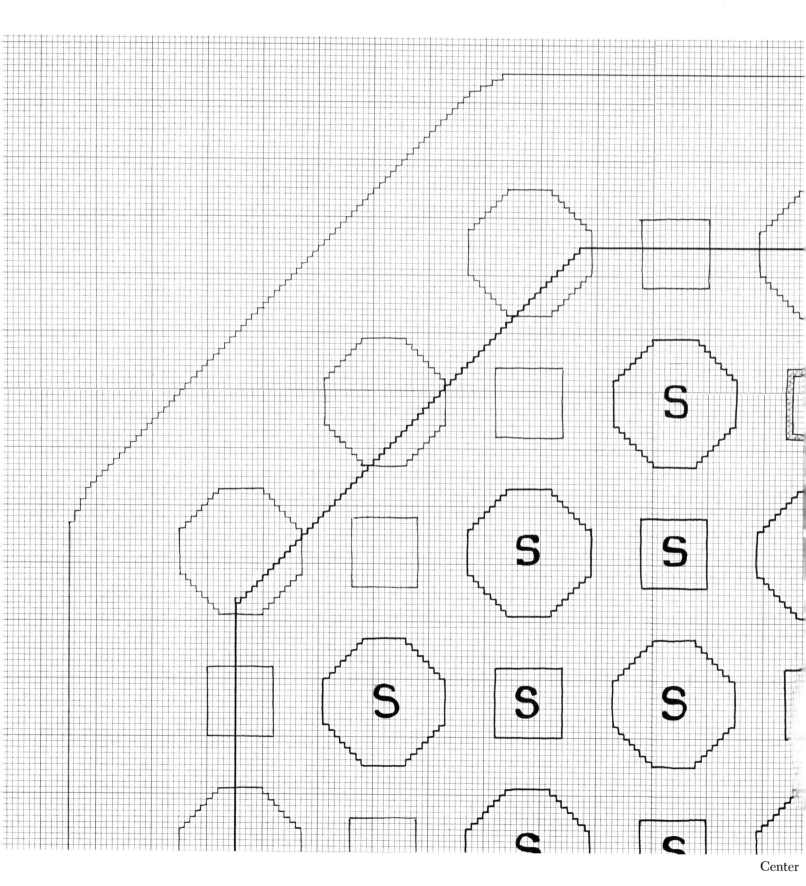

measures 27″. For the smaller rug, use the motifs marked "S."
For the larger one you should add the other motifs. If you
wanted only the motifs, as for the smaller rug, your center
background could be done as far as the inner outline and then
another shade or color could be used from there to the outer line
as a border. (See plate 5.)

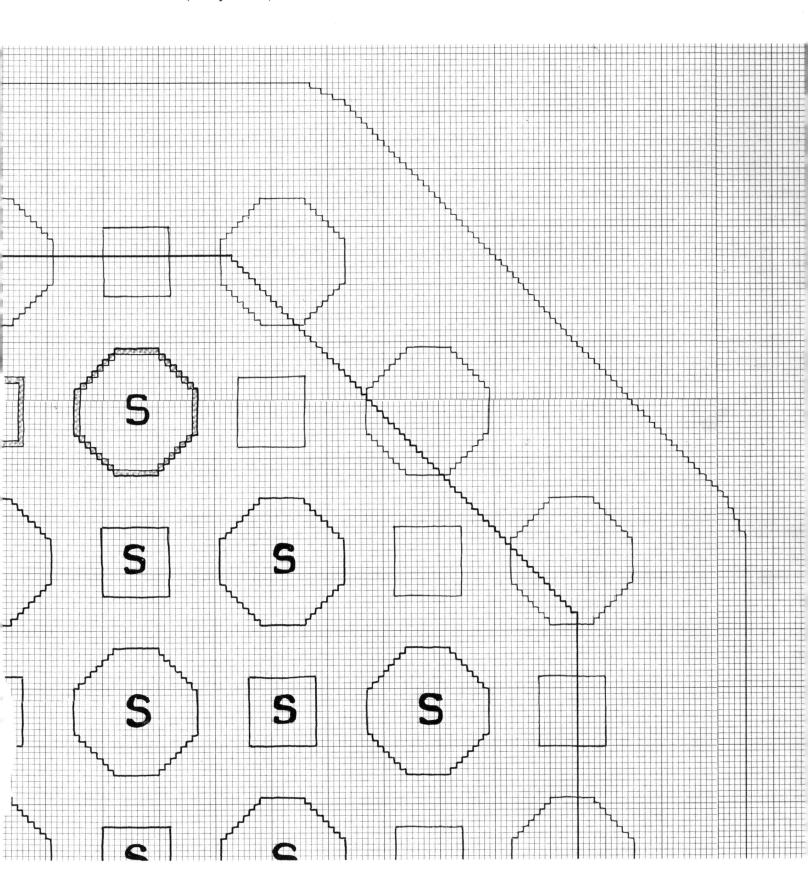

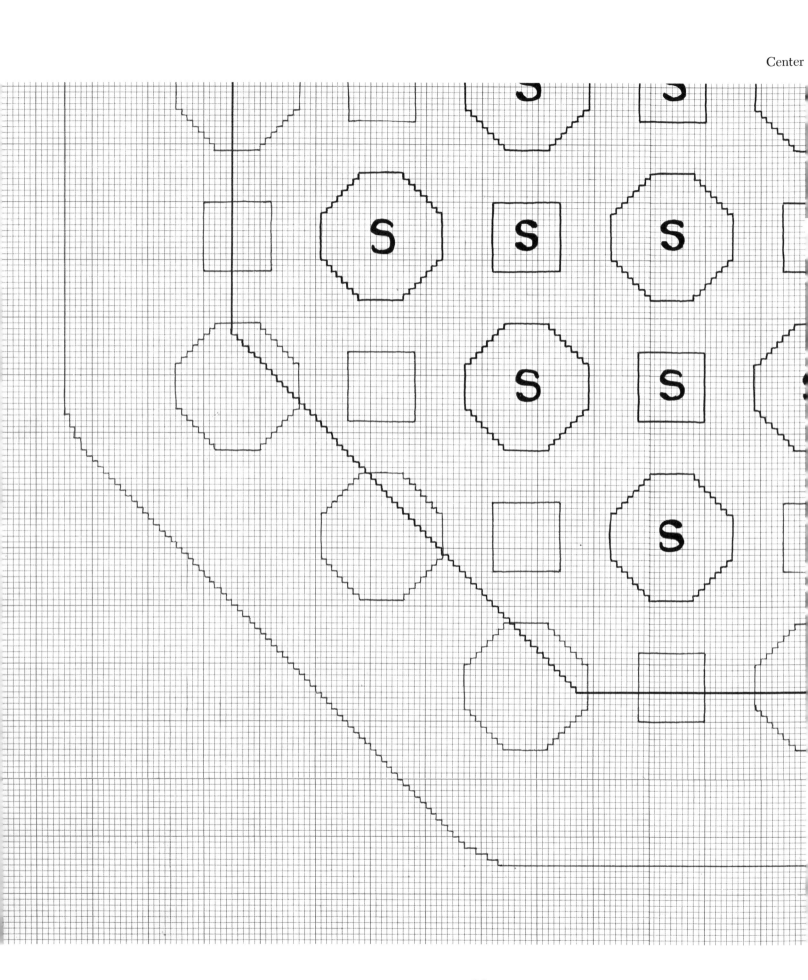

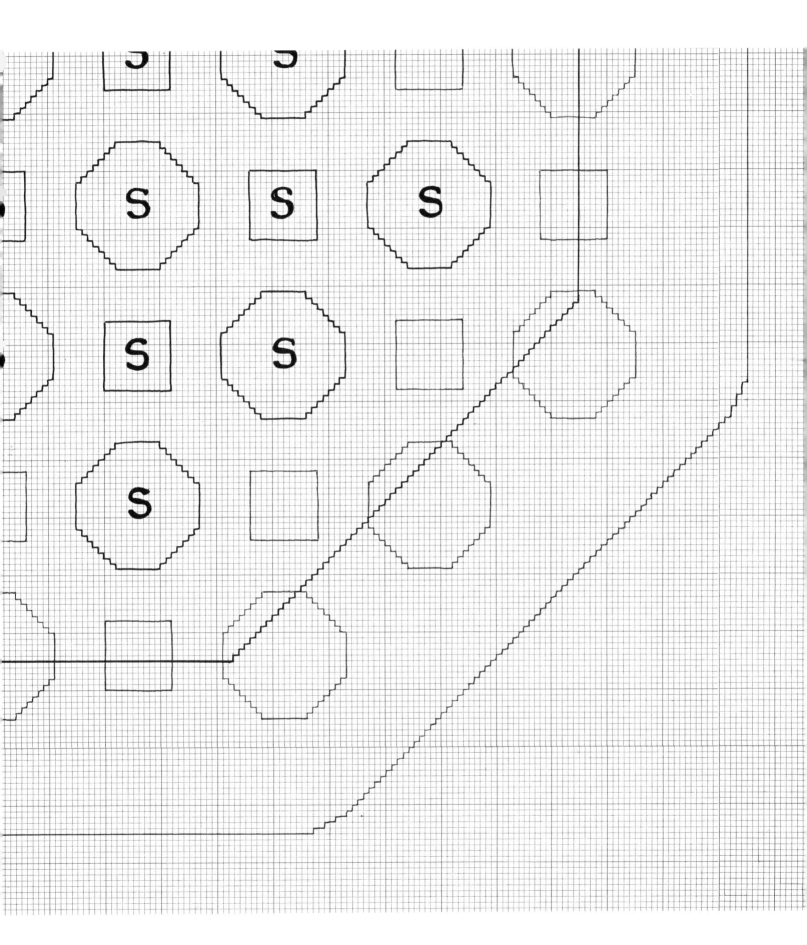

To start stitching, find the center of your canvas by either measuring or counting, and then work the center octagon. From there count out to a square next to it and work that, and so on. I outlined the squares and octagons in brown except for the center octagon, which is solid brown. The next four are orange, the four outside of those are gold, and the outer ones are a medium reddish brown. The squares are filled in with teal.

The six small motifs, shown below in a group, suggest other ways of filling in the octagons. Two have been rounded and could replace the octagon shape.

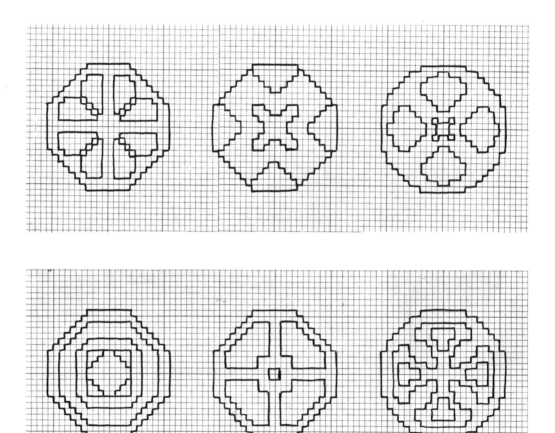

Red and Green Hexagon Design

38″ by 51″ on 12-mesh canvas
46″ by 62″ on 10-mesh canvas

This is an adaptation of an Isfahan rug shown only in black and white in *The Connoisseur's Guide to Oriental Carpets*. It was described as having 8 colors: "2 reds, 1 blue, 1 green, 1 white, 1 orange, 1 black, and 1 brown." The origin is Iran, in the Kerman region. While the rug was being stitched, most people who saw it thought it was an American Indian design. I should think it would fit very well with our Indian rugs. (See plate 6.)

The rug was worked on 12-mesh canvas, using Nantucket Needlework yarn except for the green and bright red, which are Paterna Persian. We used the Nantucket yarn as it comes but used only two strands of the Persian. It is 457 stitches wide by 619 stitches long.

At least seven people have worked on this rug. They tried to keep track of the amounts of yarn used, but some of the little tags got away. We used approximately the following amounts: Persian R10 bright red 8 ounces, 591 green 12 ounces, Nantucket 120 black 1 ounce, 21 brown 3 ounces, 33A dark red 5 ounces, 24 orange red 6 ounces, 54 light blue 2 ounces, and off-white 3 ounces.

The bright red and dark red blocks alternate and the coloring of the figures in the green blocks alternates.

To begin stitching, count the canvas threads to find the center of a short side, then count up for the entire border. The center stitch beyond the border is the middle of the five dark red stitches. Start stitching the black line on either side of the red stitches. We found it best to do all of the hexagon borders first and then the figures within them. Of course, once you have a figure done you can start working that background color.

You can easily enlarge this design by adding more of the hexagons in the width, the length, or both. To change the length of the borders to fit a larger rug, always start in the center of a side and work to each corner. You will have to make adjustments in the corners.

Dotted lines on graphs indicate pattern overlap.

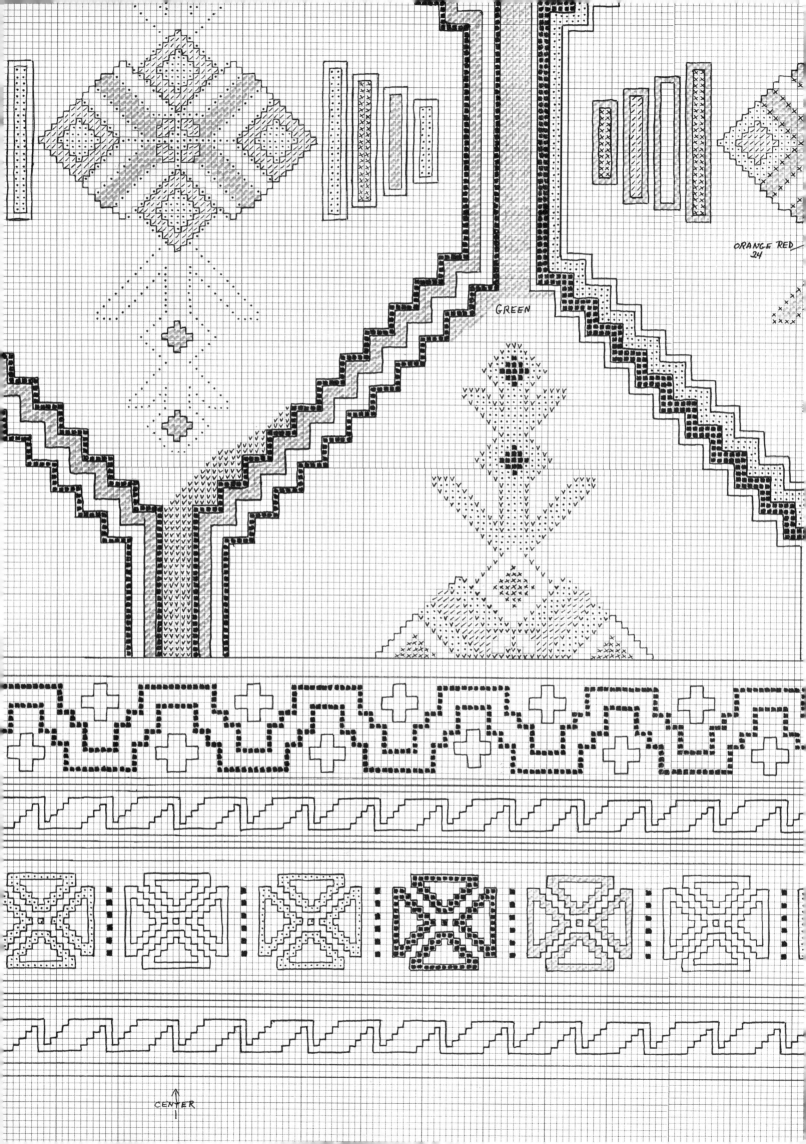

ORANGE RED
24

GREEN

CENTER

BROWN 21

GREEN

OFF WHITE

GREEN 591

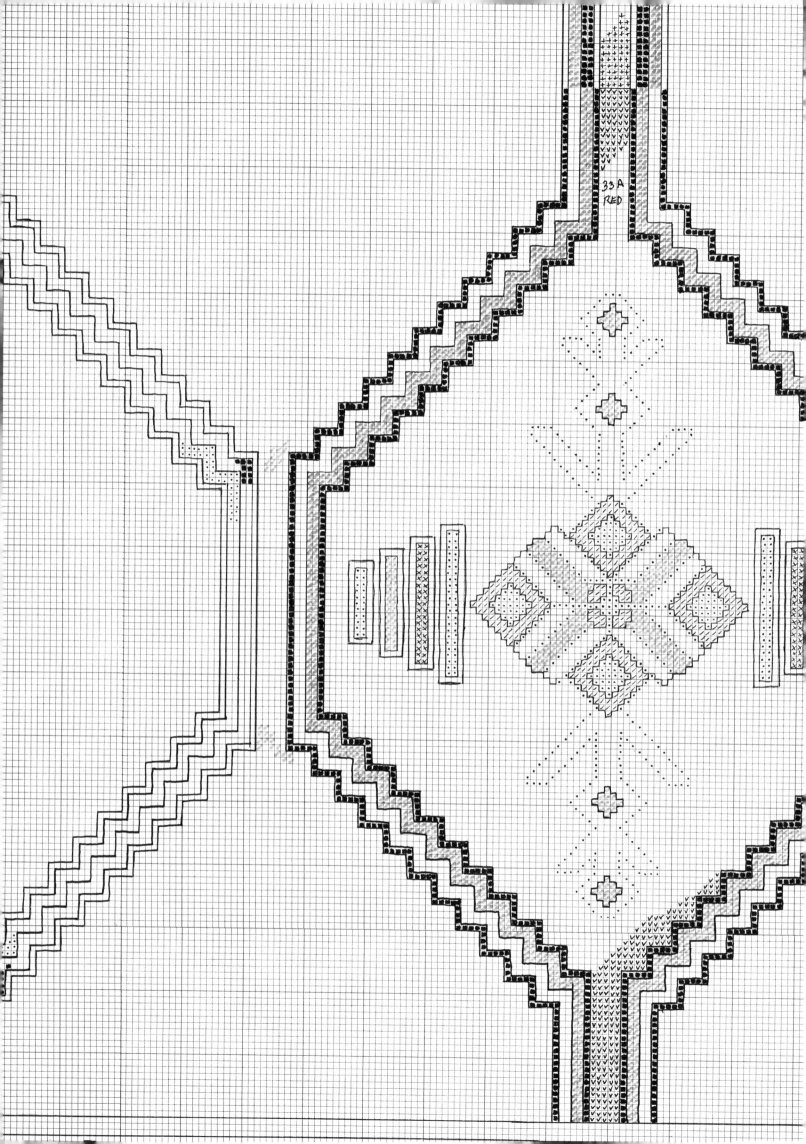

R 10
RED

BLACK

OFF WHITE

LT BLUE
54

BROWN 21

GREEN

OFF WHITE

ORANGE RED
24

GREEN

GREEN 591

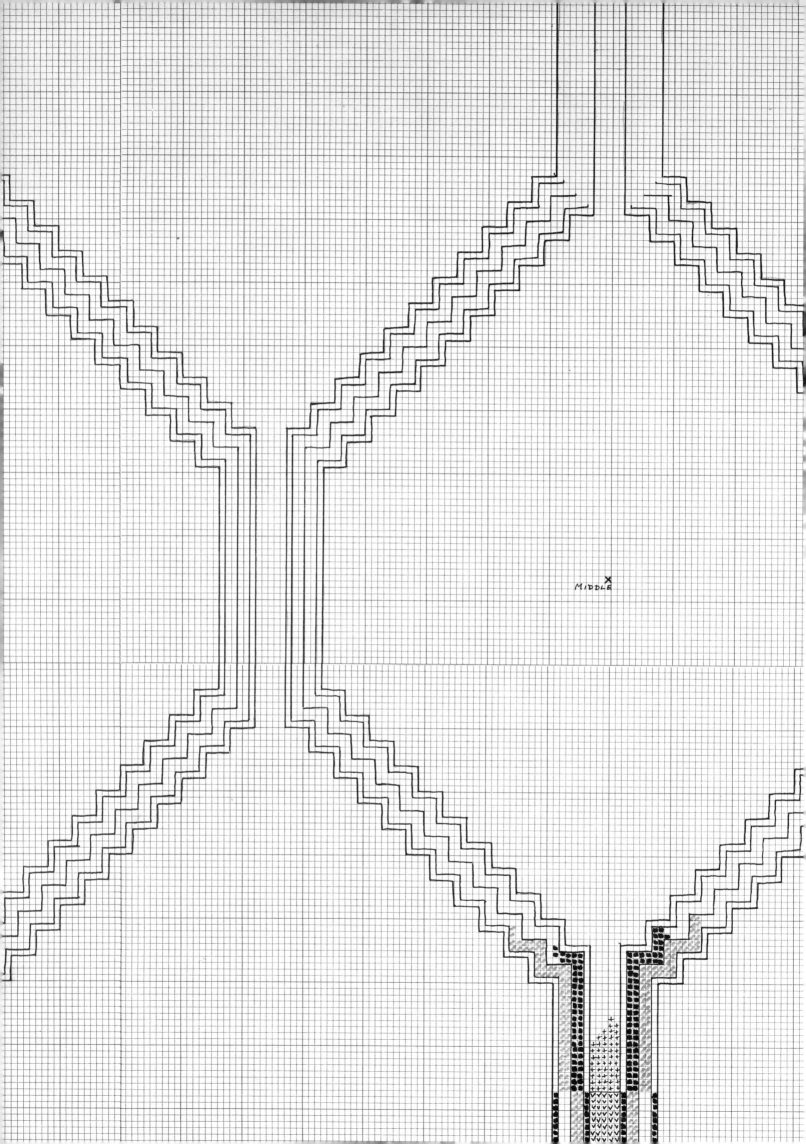

Iranian Multiblock rug

46½" by 59¼"

This is one of the rugs that we photographed in the rug department of Liberty's of London. The rug is woven of a silk pile. The size is 4' 5" by 6' 9" and at the time we were there, in May 1974, the price was approximately $7,500. The colors were beige, aqua, gold, rust, and black. (See plates 7 and 8.)

I have charted six of the assorted designs, which can be arranged in many ways:

1. Take one of the designs on pages 36 and 37, for instance, and make a rug of four blocks. For the top left block use the design as charted; for the top right block, flip it over (back to back). For the lower blocks, flip the two top ones over (bottom to bottom). The design will be facing in four directions.
2. Use only two designs alternately, for as large a rug as you wish.
3. The background of a design can be varied by changing any part of the design of that color next to the background to one of the other colors.
4. A runner could be made by using two blocks wide and as many in length as needed.

On 10-mesh canvas, each block, including one border, measures 12" by 16¼", so each row of blocks added widthwise will make a rug 12" wider and each row of blocks added lengthwise will make a rug 16¼" longer. The chart, as shown, with nine blocks (three by three) measures 46½" by 59¼". Four blocks (two by two) would measure 34¼" by 42¾".

The windowpaning border fits nicely, so that no matter how many blocks you use it will work out the same. The outer borders will vary at the corners. These should be started at the center of each side and worked toward the corners, where you must make some adjustment. Try a few variations on a piece of graph paper and find what you like.

To start this pattern, I would suggest that you set up the outline of all of your blocks, being sure to center the pattern on your canvas. This is best done by counting. Then you can fill in each block as you choose. The windowpaning borders would come next, then each outer border in order.

The background of the windowpaning border is beige with the design done in black, rust, and gold. The two borders of V's and dashes are also on a ground of beige with the design in aqua, rust, and gold. The wider border has a ground of gold; vines of black and aqua; flowers outlined in black with aqua, rust, and beige centers.

The doll-house rug shown in plate 9 is graphed on page 37. Instead of black we used 114 rich brown, and the other colors were 145 medium golden brown, 496 pale gold, and 793 aqua. It was worked on 18-mesh canvas using one strand of Persian yarn. It measures 7½″ by 9¾″.

If this same design was worked in the latch hook method it would measure approximately 36″ by 43″. Be sure to buy more canvas than you think you need, because it varies anywhere from 3½ to 4 mesh per inch and this can make quite a difference in the finished size.

Section of Multiblock

Liberty Doll-House Rug

Doll-House Rug

Patchwork Medallion—Liberty's

7′ 2″ by 10′ 3″ on 10-mesh canvas

This is a very unusual Iranian rug, which was woven of silk. The size of the original is 4′ 8″ by 7′ 3″. There were 14 to 15 knots to an inch. In order to work out all the small patterns on 10-mesh canvas, the rug grew to 7′ 2″ by 10′ 3″. On 14-mesh it would be nearer to the original size. See plate 10.

The rug would have to be done in three full-length strips, one for the center including the end borders, and one for each of the side borders. Leave off one row of the side borders for stitching after they are seamed to the center. Use three strands of Persian yarn for 10-mesh, two strands for 14-mesh.

Another way of adding borders is to work an extra row on the two sides to be joined (instead of leaving off one row on one of the sides). Then sew between the extra row and the row that ends the design to join (the extra row will be turned back on the wrong side).

The colors in the original rug were 211 rose-red background, 433 gold, off-white, 765 aqua, 410 rust, and black. I have added 405, a darker rust, on the chart.

Dotted lines on graphs indicate pattern overlap.

Bottom left and upper right corners
(reverse for other two corners)

41

Bottom left and upper right corners   (reverse for other two corners)

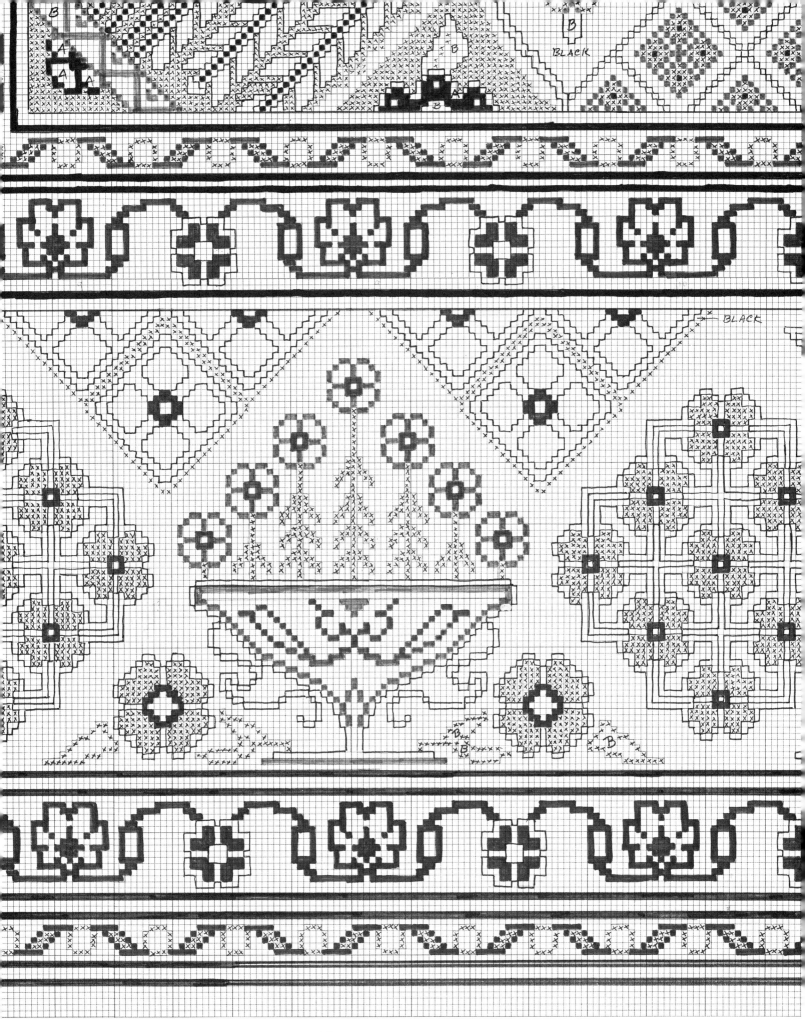

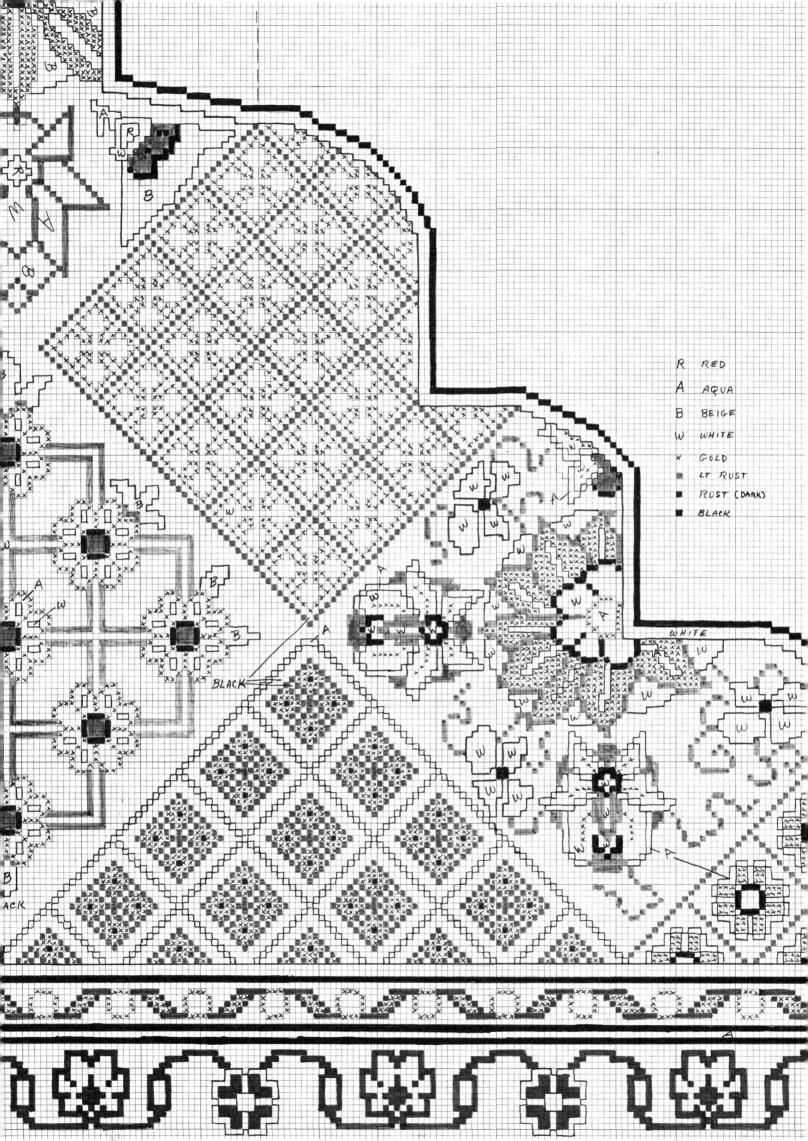

R RED
A AQUA
B BEIGE
W WHITE
x GOLD
▪ LT RUST
▪ RUST (DARK)
■ BLACK

WHITE

BLACK

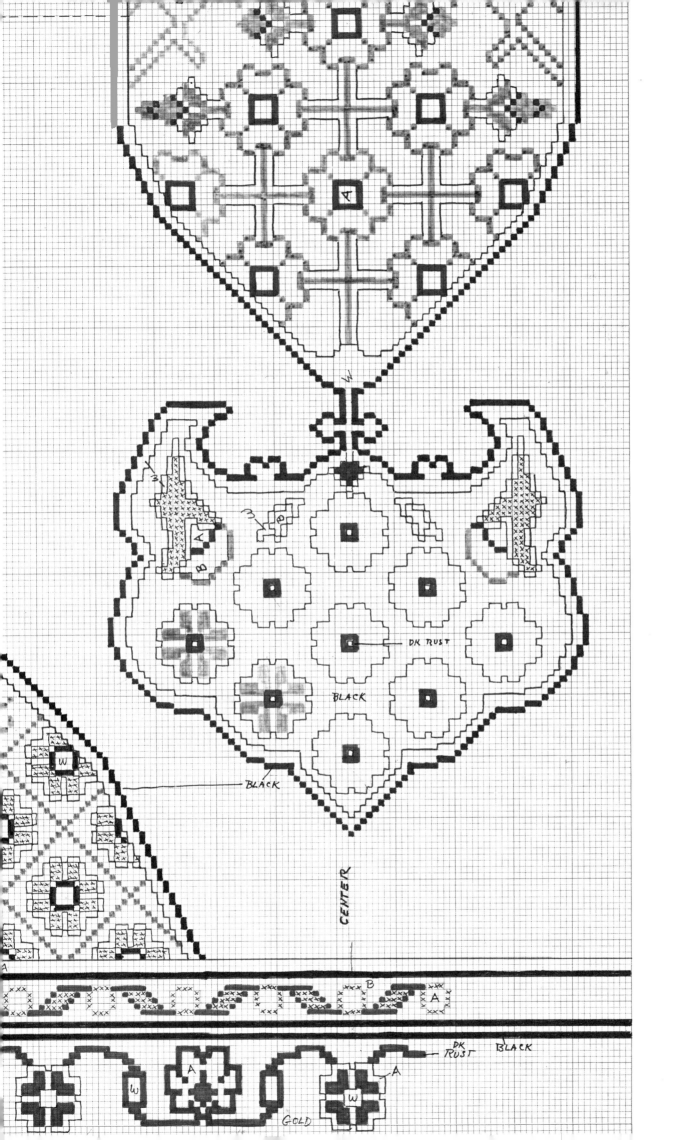

A

W

B

A

B

DK RUST

BLACK

BLACK

CENTER

W

B

A

DK
RUST

BLACK

A

A

W

W

GOLD

Caucasian (Kuba)
Nineteenth Century

35″ by 58¼″ on 10-mesh canvas

Plate 11 shows a portion of the rug photographed at the Victoria and Albert Museum. The chart is an adaptation of this rug. I have made changes in order to give a little more symmetry to the pattern.

All the small squares in the narrow borders have gold centers and red lines. Every other section is dark blue and the alternate sections are light blue, medium blue, gold, or cream as indicated. One long edge has the colors marked. Do the other edge to match.

In the wider border all the squares have gold centers and red lines, but all sections are dark blue.

The round motifs on each of the narrow sides are slightly different from those on the long sides. The motifs on one short side are color keyed. At the opposite end, the colors will be the same, but have just exchanged places. On the long sides, follow through as indicated.

The center border is outlined with red and filled in with gold. The interior repeats the first few rows as established. However, at about the middle, the spacing of the heart shape over the small diamond has been increased by one.

The dark borders and the background of the center is dark blue. The narrow borders and the background of the borders with just the squares is red, and the wide border is cream.

If you would like a lighter look, the dark blues could be changed to a medium blue and the red lightened to a rose. Then the little designs in the middle could alternate, rose and cream or rose and gold.

To make the rug on 10-mesh canvas you will need 5½′ of 40″ canvas.

To start, find the center of the short edge of the canvas about 3″ in from the end. An arrow marks the center stitch of the border. There are 164 stitches on each side of the center stitch, 329 total stitches across.

Dotted lines on graphs indicate pattern overlap.

Photograph shows top section of rug; chart shows from the bottom up

GOLD

DARK BLUE

RED

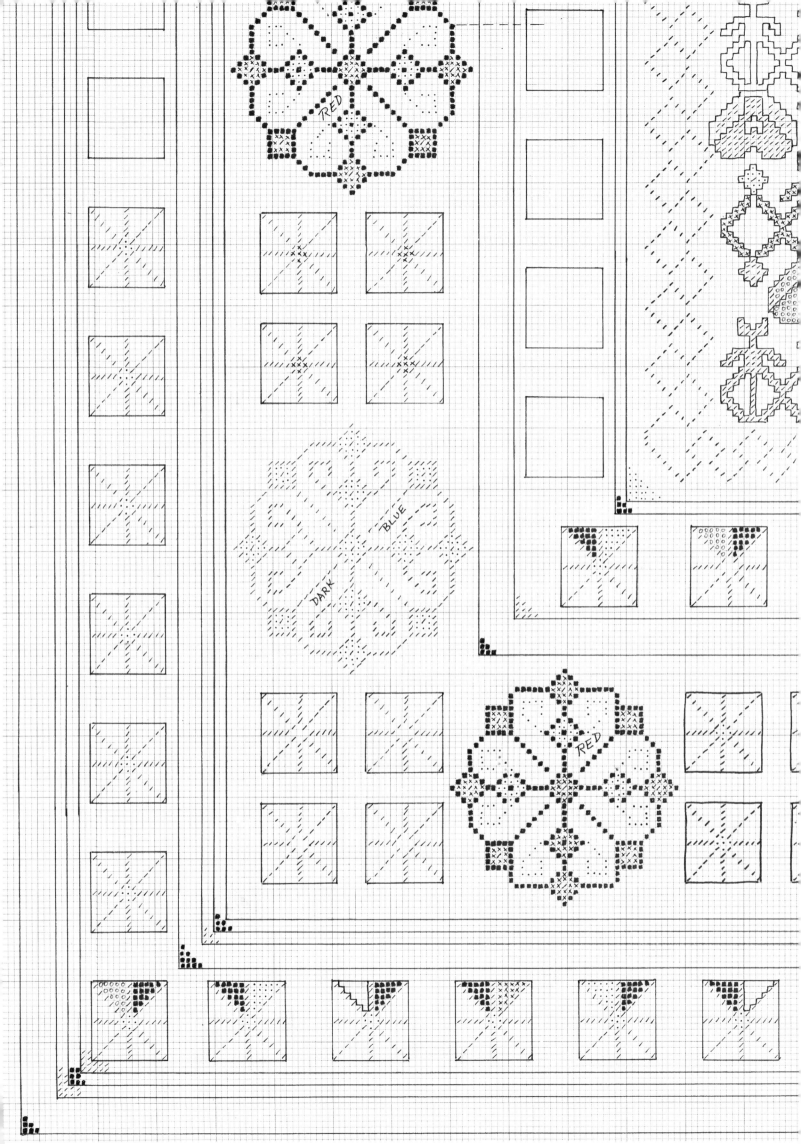

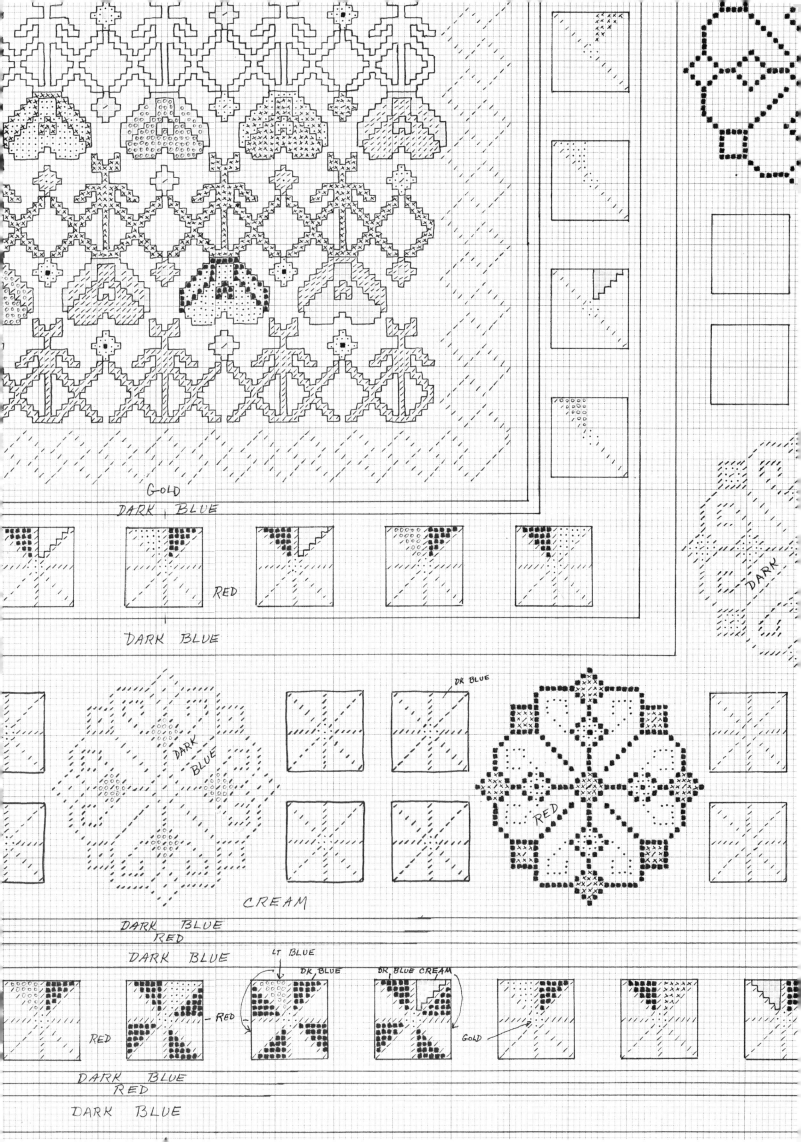

GOLD

DARK BLUE

RED

DARK BLUE

DARK BLUE

DK BLUE

DARK BLUE

CREAM

RED

DARK BLUE
RED

DARK BLUE

LT BLUE

DK BLUE

DK BLUE CREAM

RED

RED

GOLD

DARK BLUE
RED

DARK BLUE

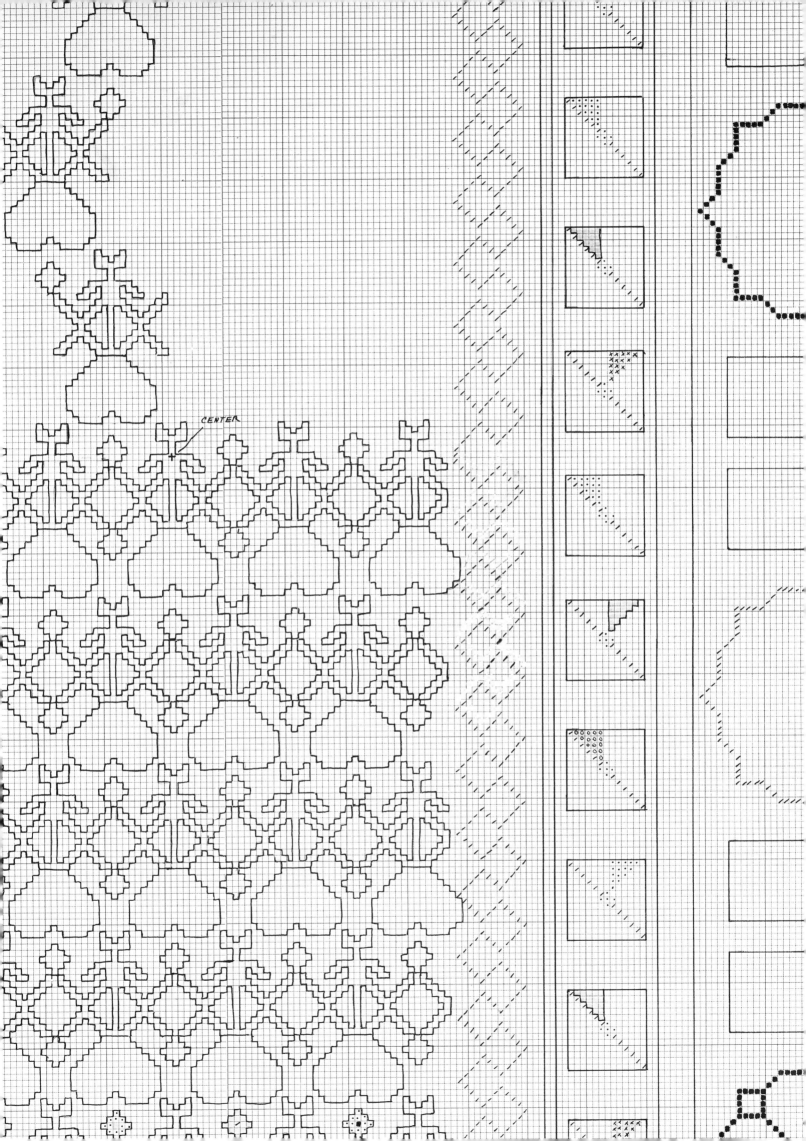

CENTER

Pink Samarkand

66½" by 114½" on 10-mesh canvas
(5' 6½" by 9' 6½")

Since, as of this writing, the widest 10-mesh canvas available is 60", this rug has to be pieced. The best place to do this would be at the end of the black stitches of the fret border. This would be a center strip of a 51" worked area. Leaving a row of the white border to be worked when joining, the side strips would be about 7½" wide. You should purchase about 7 yards of canvas 60" wide from the same roll. Half the length will be for the center panel and you will cut two strips 12" wide for the side borders. This allows about 6" at each end. See plate 12.

This rug can be made narrower to just fit on the 60" canvas. By eliminating one whole fret design (on the short side) and starting right in the corner instead of leaving the extra 12 stitches, the width will be cut by 78 stitches or 6½"—3¼" on each end. I have redesigned the flower and cloud borders (separate chart) to fit this shorter width. A different part of the cloud border is now at the center. The outside white, pink, and gray borders would have to be eliminated.

In the field of the rug, the medallions that line up in the center would remain as they are, but all the side medallions would have 19 stitches less on one side and 20 stitches less on the opposite side of each one. The corner triangles would remain as they are, which of course would make them closer together. Please pay attention to the slight variations in the count of the fret border and the cloud border. Check them as you do them.

The yarns used in my sample were dyed with natural dyes. The pink main color was unmordanted yarn in a bath of cochineal and a little fustic. The pale pink was unmordanted dyed in cochineal. The aqua was unmordanted dyed in indigo and overdyed in fustic. The gray and black were chrome mordanted and dyed in logwood. The yellow was unmordanted dyed in marigold blossoms.

I used black yarn, but I think a very dark indigo (navy) was probably used in the original rug. Since doing this pattern, I have seen this type of rug with a bright yellow background and another with a bright blue background.

The design source of this rug is *All Color Book of Oriental Carpets and Rugs* by Stanley Reed.

Please note that the corner of the cloud border and the flower border on the chart is different from that shown in the colorplate. The chart shows a better-looking corner. The motifs on the chart are spread out a little more. The entire chart shows a little more than a quarter of the entire rug.

Dotted lines on graphs indicate pattern overlap.

Where the graphs say "over 1 st," move the motifs one stitch to the left to center them.

This shows just a small section of the rug as charted.

WHITE
DR PINK

LT PINK

YELLOW

QUA

DR PINK

YELLOW

PALE
PINK

AQUA   LT-   WHITE
        PINK

DK   GRAY
PINK

AQUA

OVER ← 1 ST.

AQUA

DR PINK

YELLOW

PALE
PINK

OVER ← 1 ST.

GRAY

LT PINK

WHITE

OVER ← 1 ST.

OVER ← 1 ST.

AQUA

WHITE

WHITE

GRAY

OVER ← 1 ST.

GRAY

LT PINK

WHITE

OVER ← 1 ST

BLACK

WHITE   GRAY

WHITE

GRAY

YELLOW

AQUA

BLACK

YELLOW

DK PINK

AQUA

WHITE

WHITE

GRAY

OVER ← 1 ST.

BLACK

WHITE GRAY

WHITE

GRAY

YELLOW

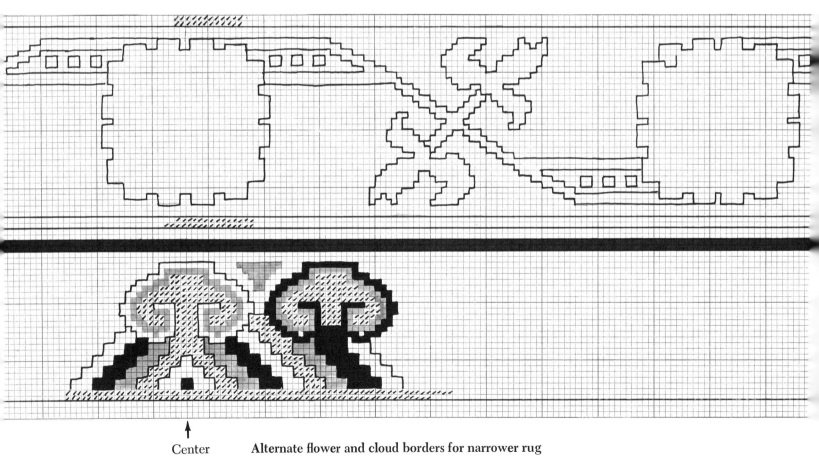

Center

Alternate flower and cloud borders for narrower rug

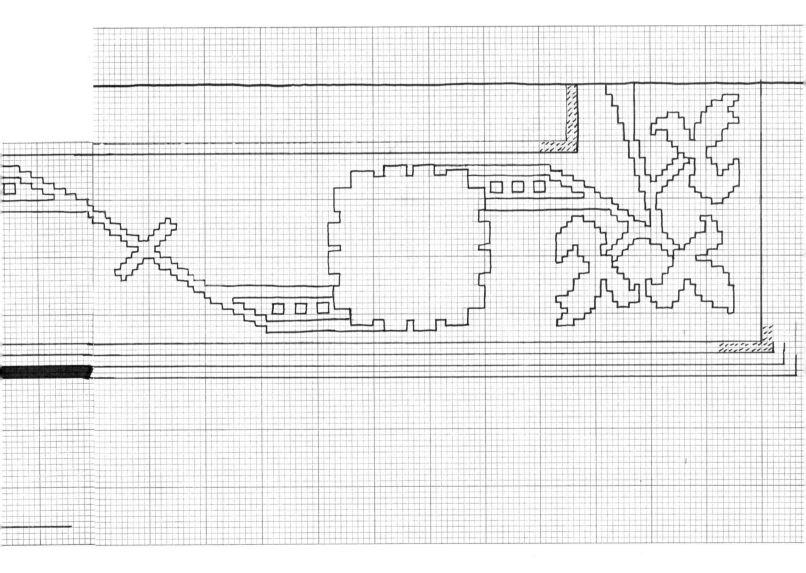

Gold Bukhara

31½″ by 63″ on 10-mesh canvas

Plates 13 and 14 show a typical Bukhara pattern in gold and two variations of borders. The large chart is given for one half of the gold version. Border variation A shows a pink and red coloring using five shades while the B variation uses four shades of blue and an off-white. The diagonal-stripe border in this version will look different on the short side than on the long side because it does not miter at the corners as the V border does in the pink one.

I have never seen Bukhara designs woven in any other colors than reds or golds, but why not use other colors if you choose?

Most of the gold colors were dyed with natural dyes. The gold was first dyed in madder with tin and cream of tartar with fustic added. The orange was unmordanted, dyed in madder, then overdyed in cochineal. The cream was unmordanted and dyed in a weak bath of fustic. The black was alum mordanted, dyed in logwood. The brown is 405 Paterna.

The Paterna colors that closely match mine are 427 gold, 419 orange, or 273 brick, 409 brown, 496 cream, and 050 black. A dark navy could replace the black. I understand that dark indigo (navy) rather than black was used in the old rugs because the dyes used for black had a tendency to rot the yarns.

Two yards of 40″ canvas would be required to make the rug as charted. Use three strands of Persian yarn.

If you would like a variation, all or part of the borders A or B could be used. They are shown in two color suggestions: A, pink; B, blue.

Dotted lines on graphs indicate pattern overlap.

Border variation A

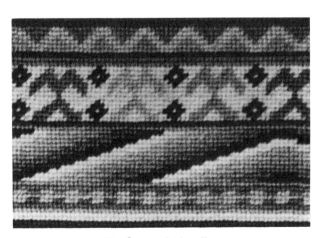

Border variation B

. 427 GOLD
o 419 ORANGE
x 409 BROWN

□ 496 CREAM
■ 050 BLACK

BOTTOM

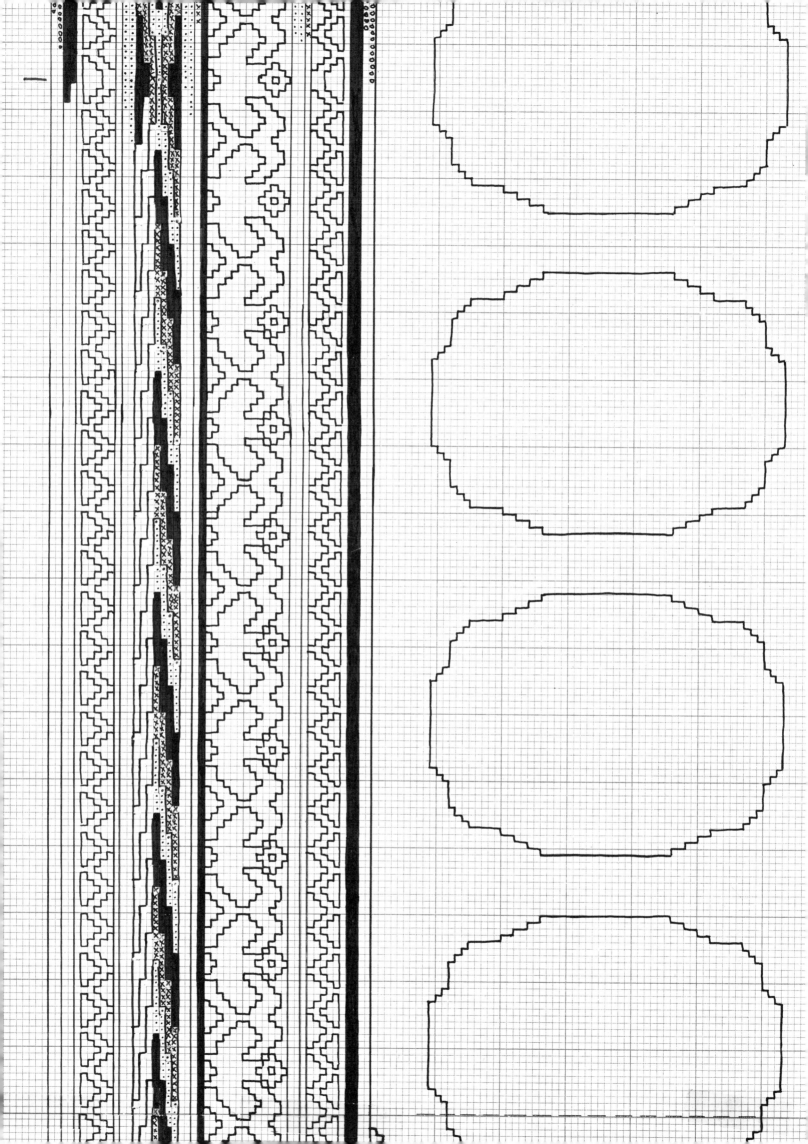

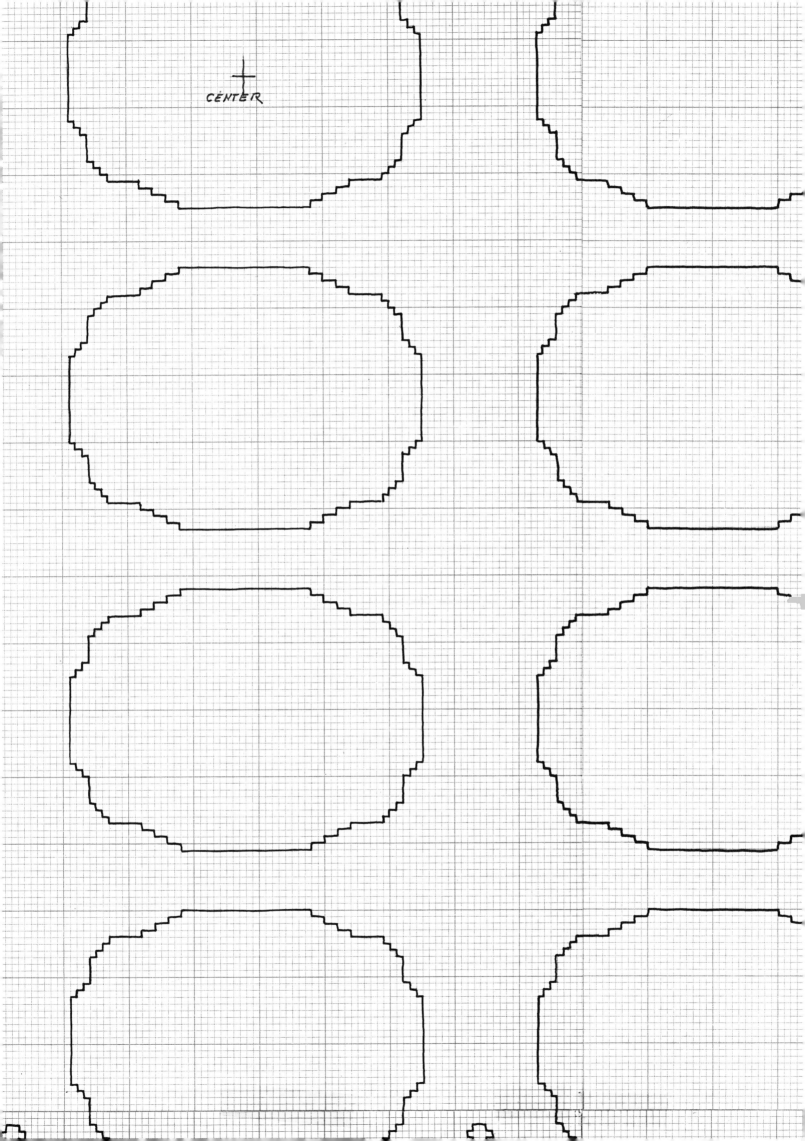

CENTER

Border variation A

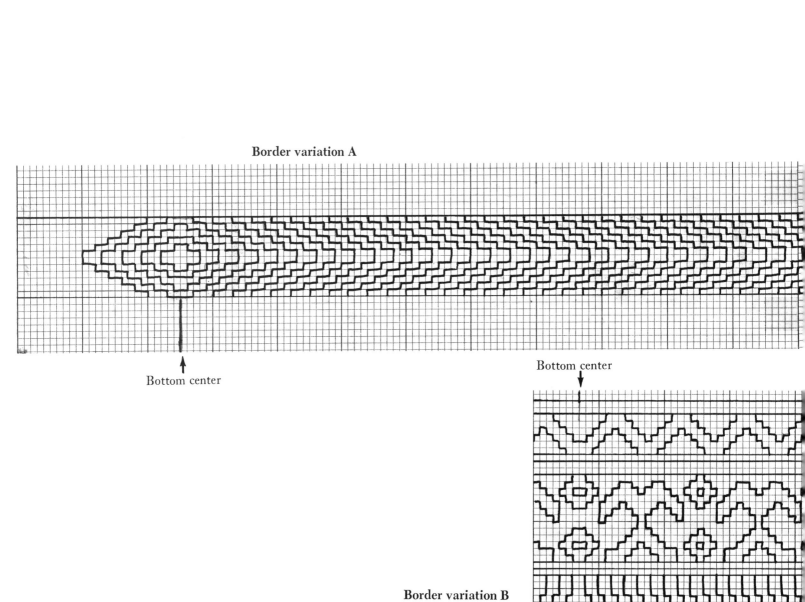

Bottom center

Bottom center

Border variation B

Center →

Center →

Repeat motif to corner

Repeat motif to corner

Red Bukhara

60″ by 87″ on 10-mesh canvas

This is a larger Bukhara design than the gold. Both of these designs could be made in either gold or red. The colors used in my sample were naturally dyed using madder, cochineal, fustic, and logwood. I tried to get the bright turkey red that is the usual red of the Bukharas but was unable to. The center background was worked with two shades of my reds, which gives a heathery look. (See plate 15.)

To use Paterna colors, I would suggest 240 bright red, 236 dark red, 210 light red, 020 cream, and 050 black or a dark navy.

To fit this on 60″ canvas, the outer X and diamond border would have to be eliminated, then each of the extreme outside single-row borders could be two rows wide.

The borders would have to be done as separate strips and seamed to the center in order to do the entire width as charted. Be sure to buy all the canvas at the same time from the same roll.

Dotted lines on graphs indicate pattern overlap.

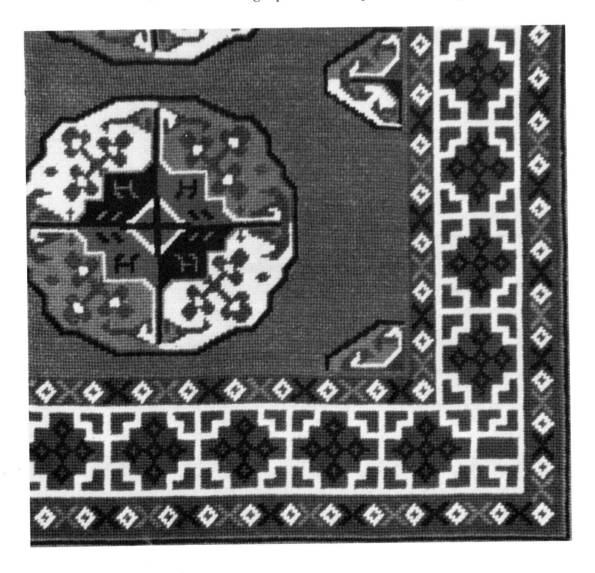

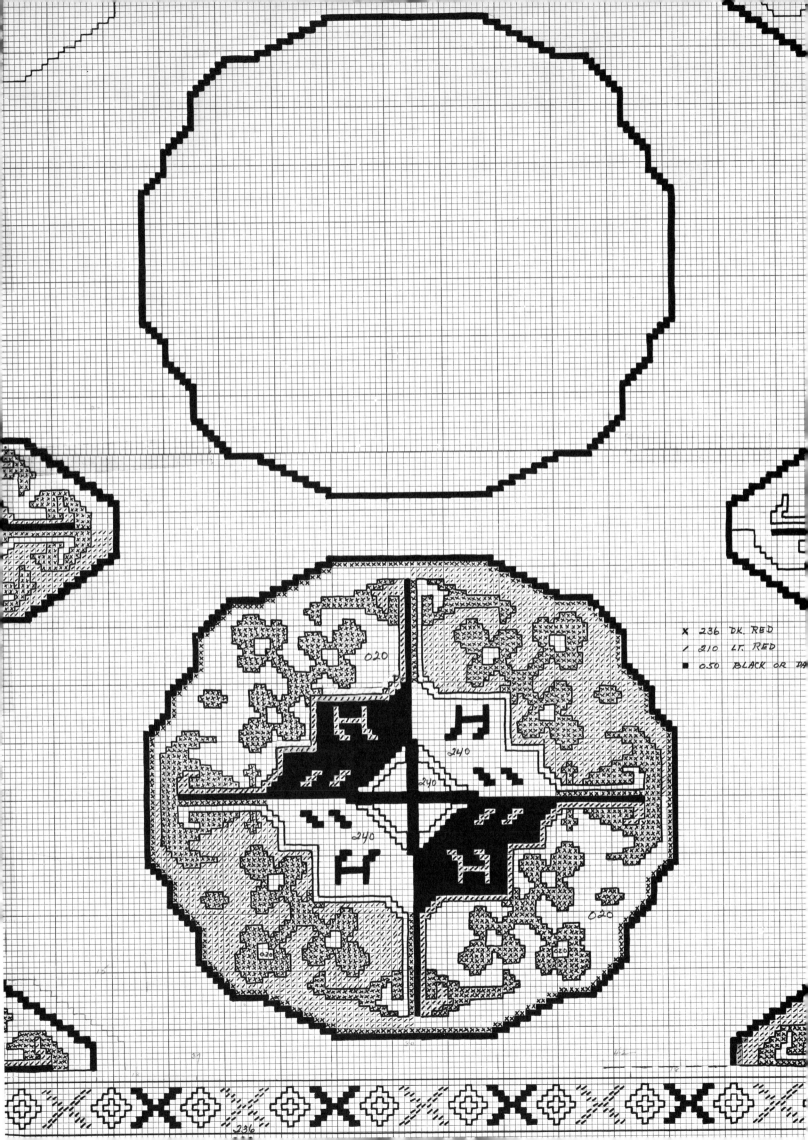

X 236 DK. RED
/ 210 LT. RED
■ 050 BLACK OR DA

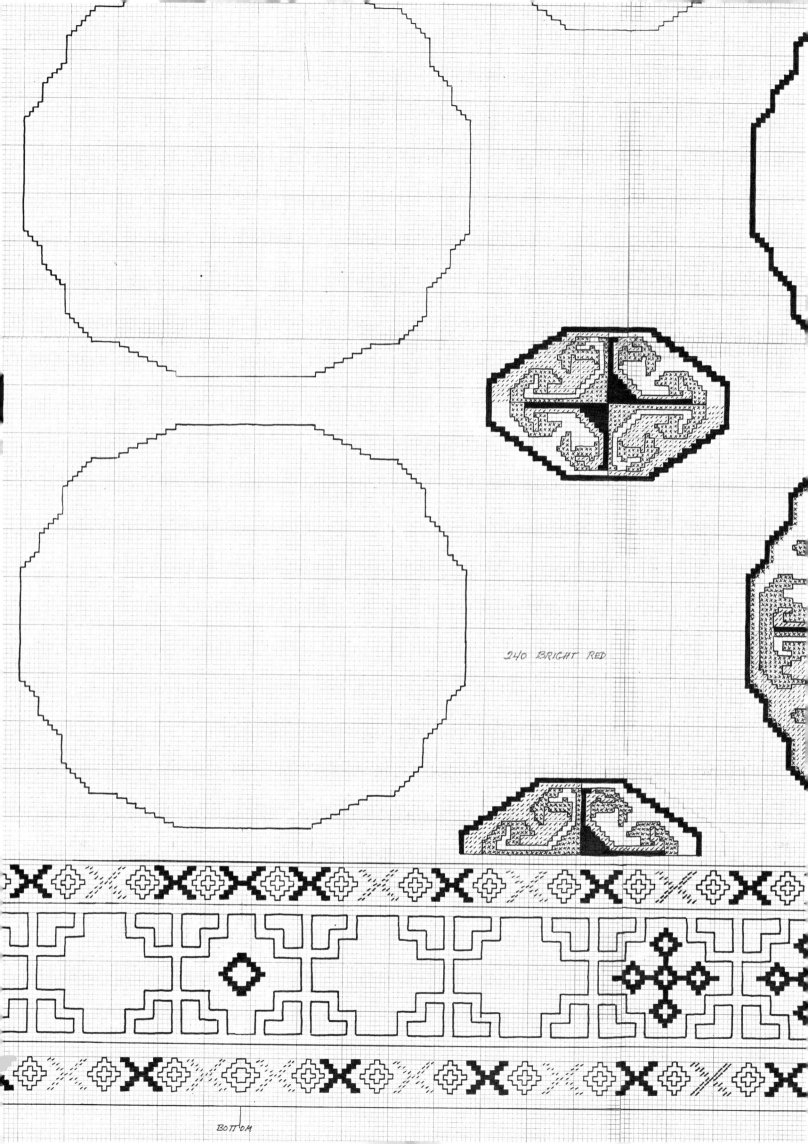

240 BRIGHT RED

BOTTOM

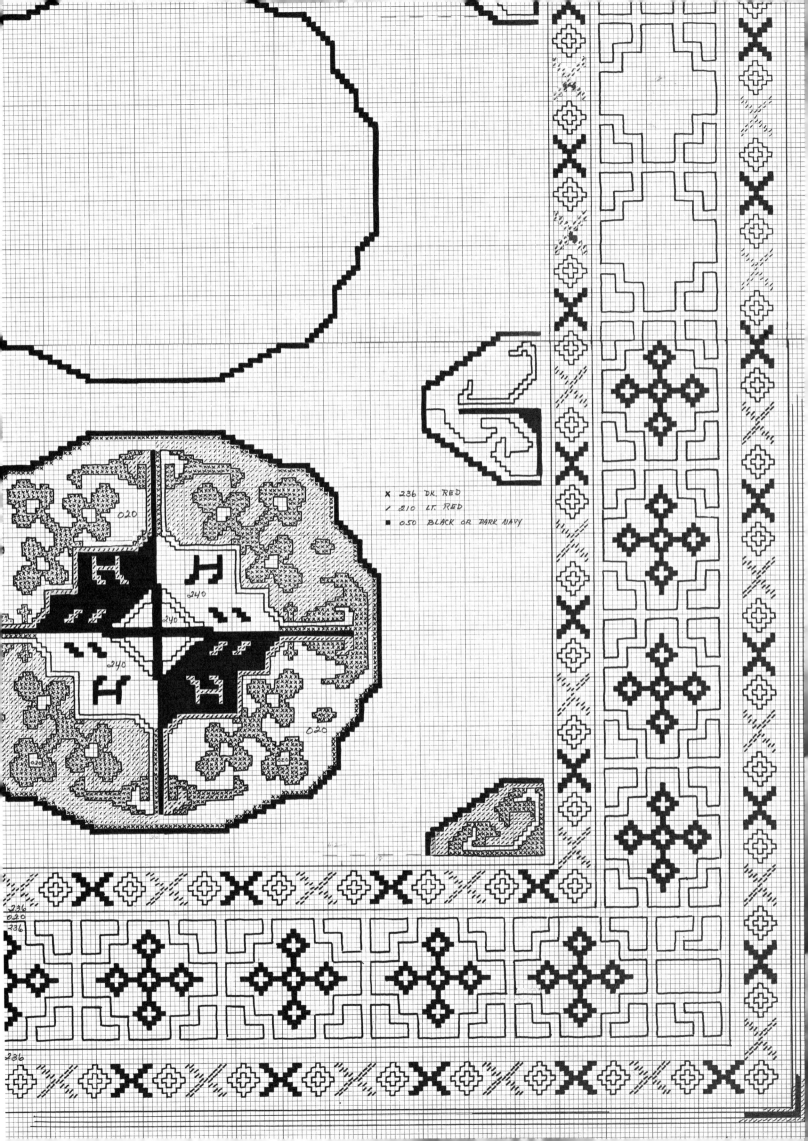

X   236   DK. RED
/   210   LT. RED
■   0.50 BLACK OR DARK NAVY

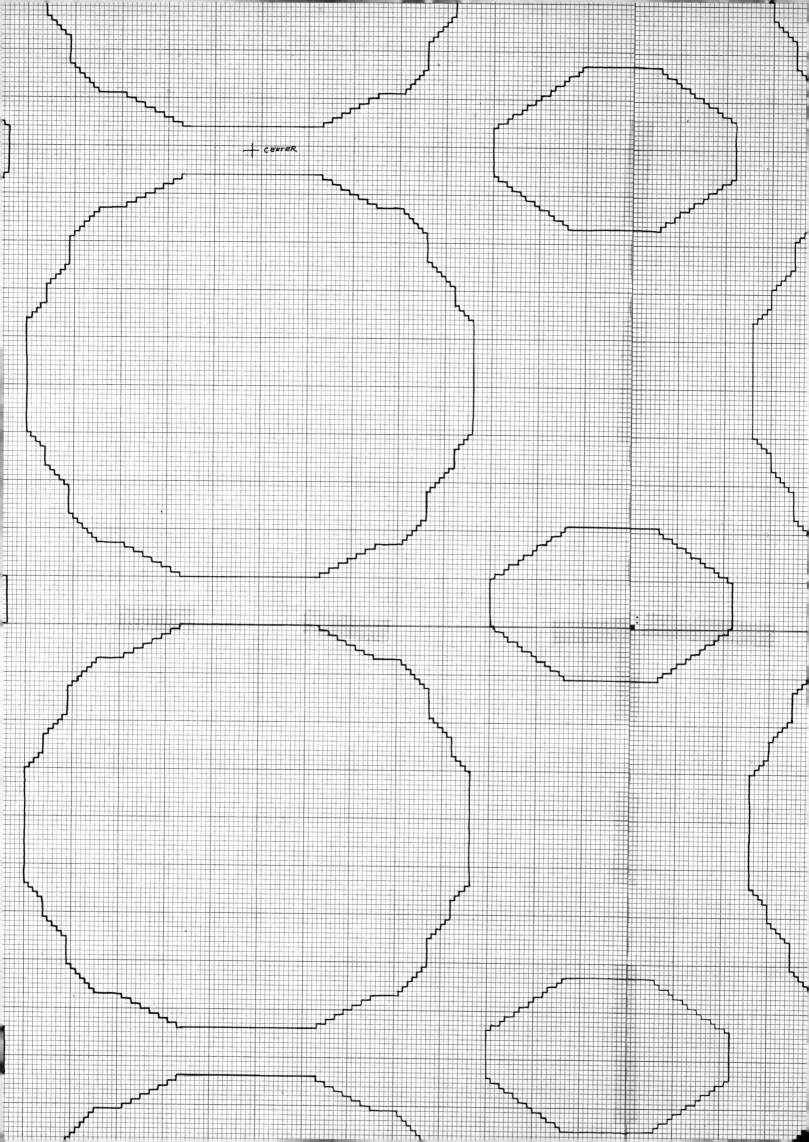

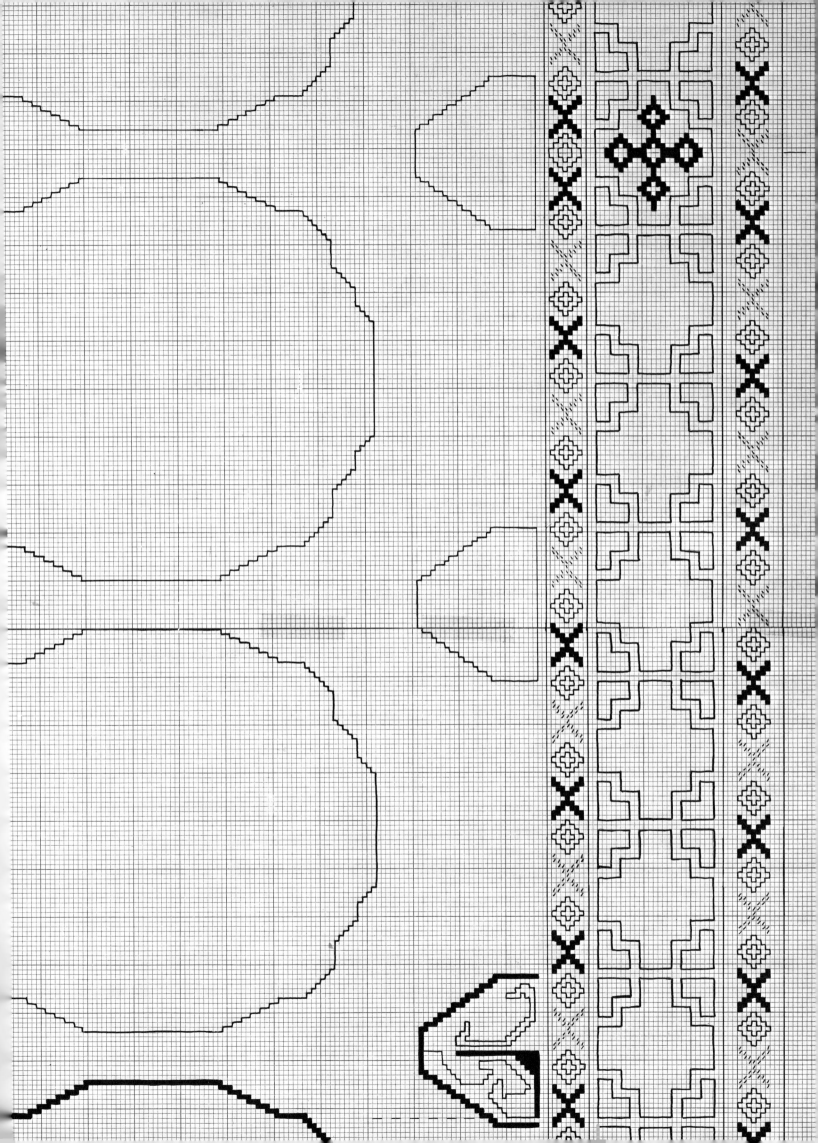

Gold and Off-White

"Alhambra Door"

29½" by 37" on 10-mesh canvas

When George and I were in Spain several years ago we visited the Alhambra in Granada. The patterns that adorned the walls, doors, and ceilings were all very beautiful. Most of them were very complicated interwoven designs. The one that I have chosen for this rug was from a carved door. I used two golds to try to simulate the gold leafing on the wood (plate 16). The design would be lovely in any two shades of a color against another color ground. Three small examples of other colors are shown. I used white with an outline of gray for plates 17 and 18. One has a bright green ground; the other has a brilliant yellow ground within the border and a medium blue for the surrounding ground area. Plate 19 shows the same gold with a brick-red background.

As charted, you would need 1 yard of 40" 10-mesh canvas. Use three strands of Persian yarn.

A 50½" by 65½" rug could be made by placing four of the interlocked borders, with the center designs, 2" apart, as shown in the diagram. This would require at least 2 yards of 60" 10-mesh canvas.

The chart, as shown, would make a rug approximately 79" by 100" if done in latch hook.

I used 433 dark gold, 531 light gold, and 012 off-white in my rug. I started it by finding the exact center and then doing the outlining of the vine and leaves in the middle. When that was finished, I did the outlining of the entire interlocked border. At this point, the lighter gold and the background were filled in within this area. Then I did the three-stitch border, and so on.

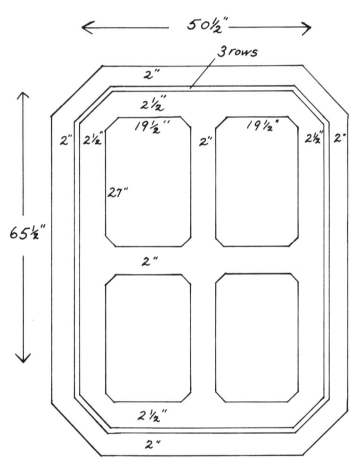

50½"

3 rows

2"

2½"

19½"

19½"

2" 2½" 2" 2½" 2" 2"

27"

65½"

2"

2½"

2"

The diagram shows the approximate
effect of repeating the interlocking
borders with the central motif four
times, then adding an outer border.

DK 74

93

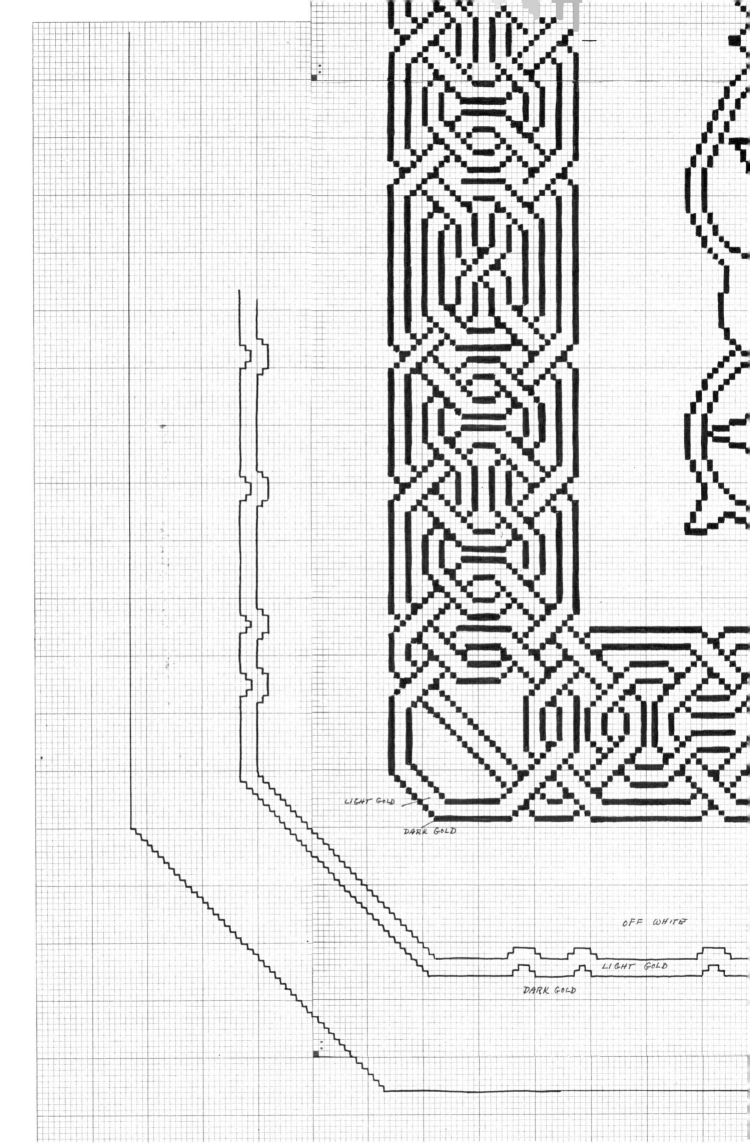

LIGHT GOLD

DARK GOLD

OFF WHITE

LIGHT GOLD

DARK GOLD

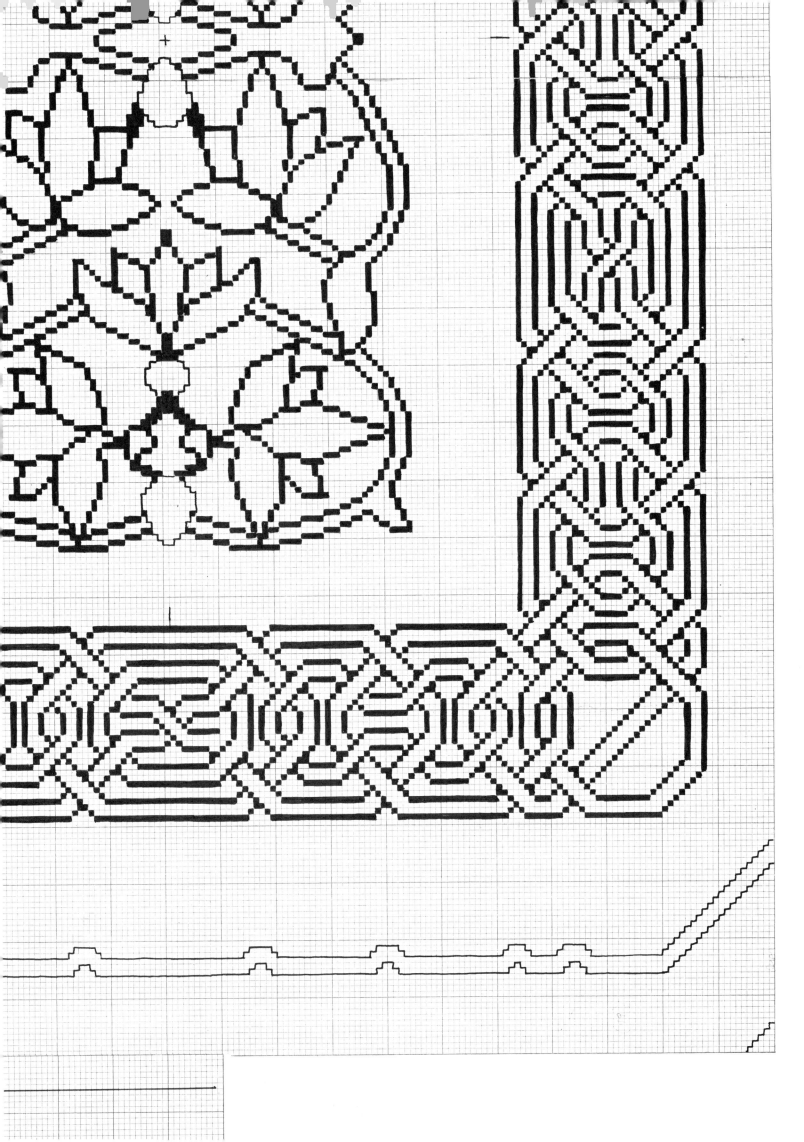

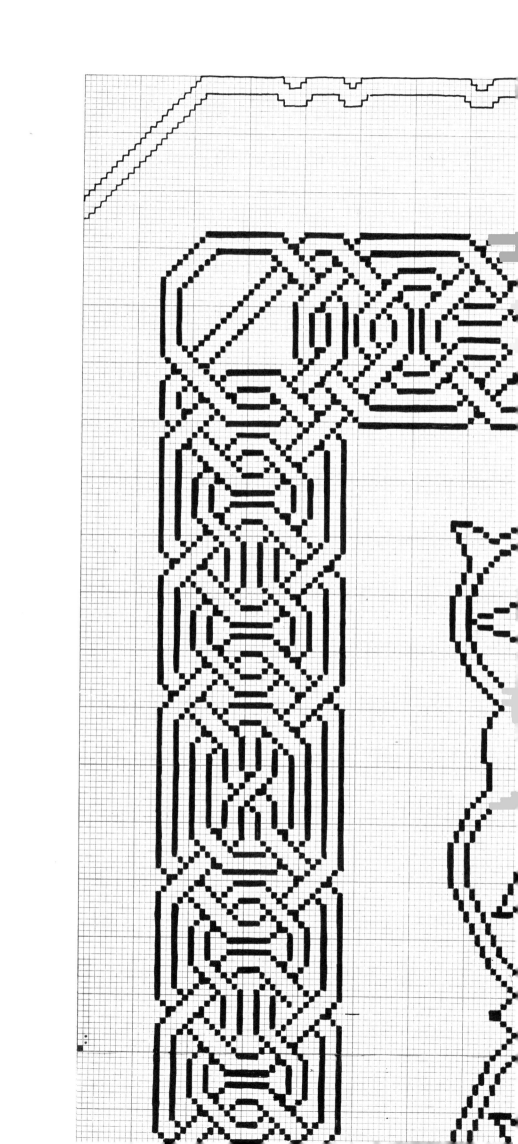

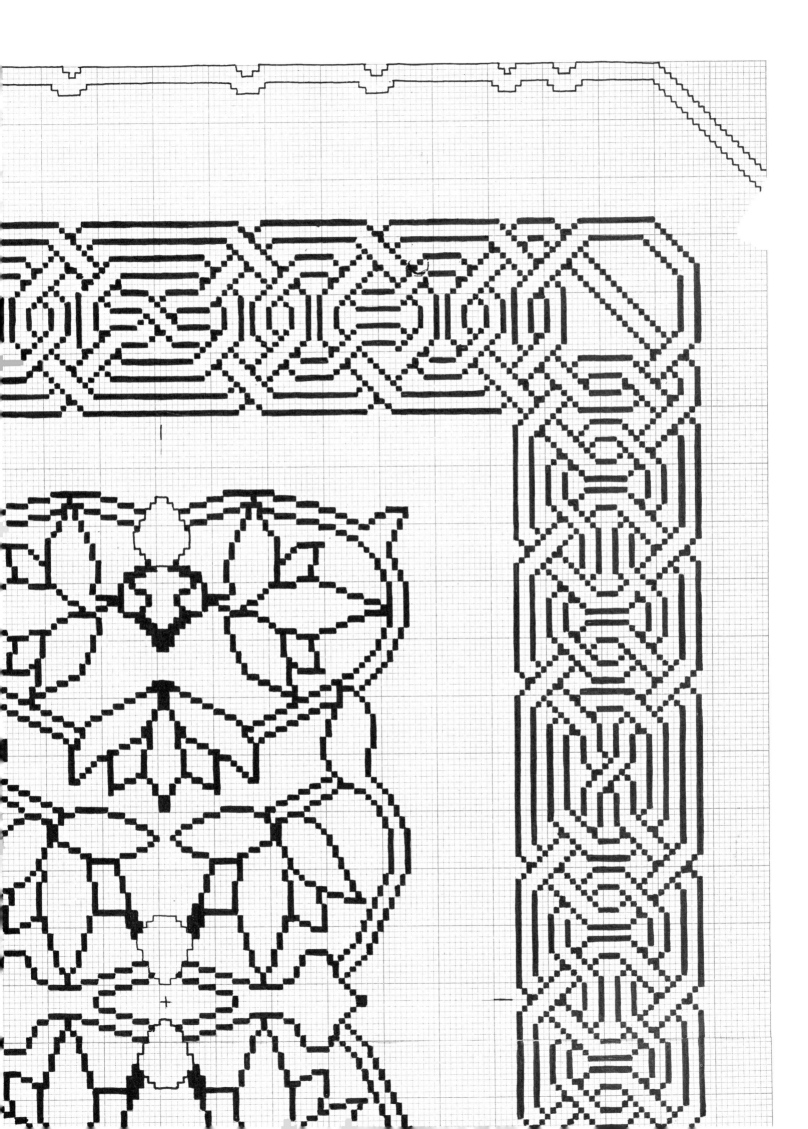

Bright Green
and Teal Moorish Design
36½" by 47" on 10-mesh canvas

The finished rug shown in colorplate 20 was worked on a painted canvas. The design had been traced on the canvas from a line drawing, which isn't always as accurate a way to have a centered design as counting from a chart. I wanted to do the bargello ground surrounding the medallion in the form of a diamond, but the medallion was not perfectly centered, so I worked at one angle only.

I used the darker of the ground blues, number 758, in tent stitch to fill in the spaces within the medallions and the corners.

The center medallion could be used alone with borders to make a smaller rug. To make a larger rug, put more space between the corner medallions where they come toward each other at the centers.

On 12-mesh canvas, the center medallion would measure about 15½" by 27", which would be a good bench design. On 14-mesh it would measure about 12¼" by 23". A latch hook rug with the entire design would measure between 92" by 118" and 98" by 125".

One and a half yards of 40" canvas would be required for this rug as charted on 10-mesh canvas. Measure carefully or count to find the center. Work the center medallion first, the corner ones next, and then the borders.

Other filling stitches could be used for the background or tent stitch entirely in one color.

718 TEAL

782 BLUE

574
GREEN

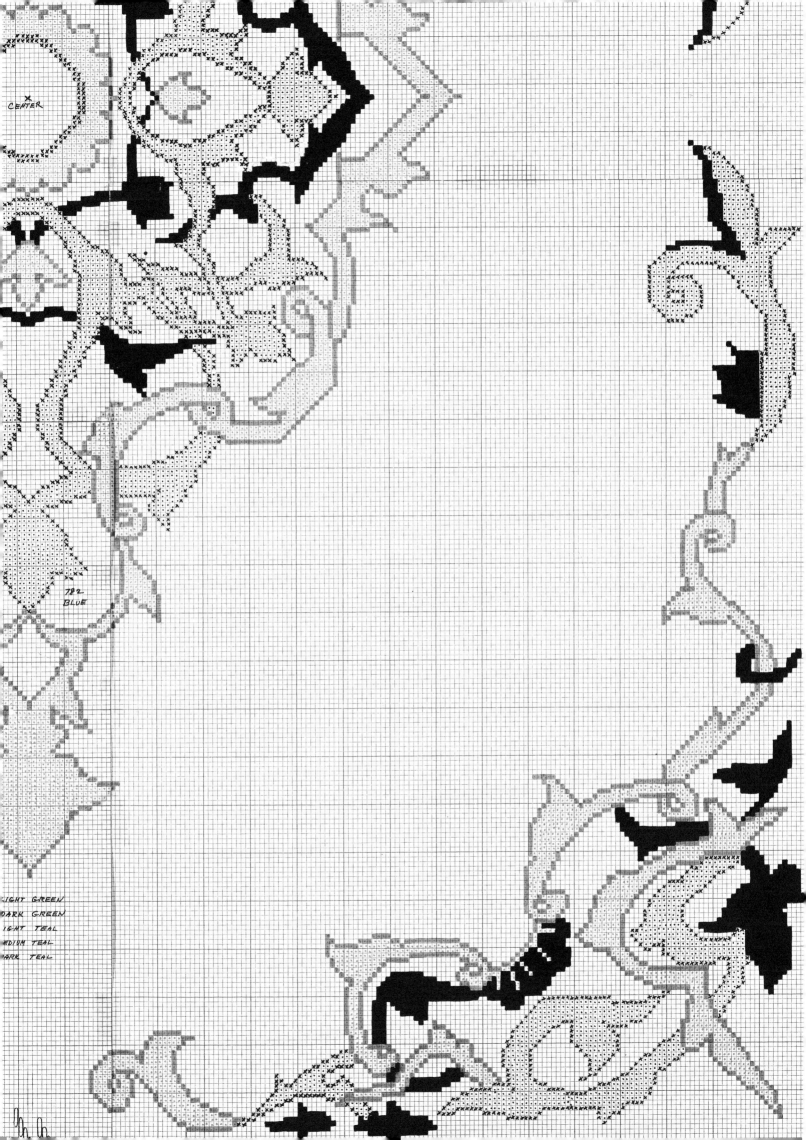

X
CENTER

782
BLUE

LIGHT GREEN
DARK GREEN
LIGHT TEAL
MEDIUM TEAL
DARK TEAL

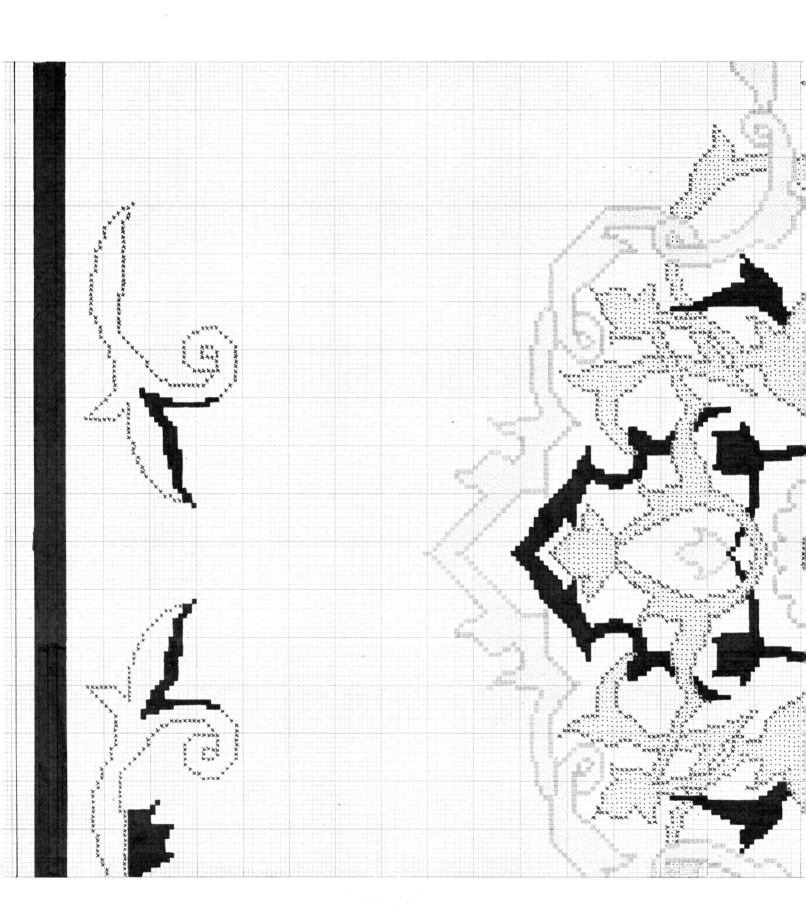

CENTER

Early Seventeenth-Century Isfahan, Persia—Period of Shah Abbas

63″ by 105″ on 10-mesh canvas

One of the books on Oriental rugs that I purchased is *Oriental Rugs in the Metropolitan Museum of Art* by M. S. Dimand and Jean Mailey. While looking through it I was stopped by the colorplate on page 145 of a silk compartment rug of the first quarter of the seventeenth century. From this photograph I charted my adaptation, using colors suitable for my foyer. (See plate 21.) It wasn't until my rug was finished that I saw the original hanging in the Islamic department at the museum. When I first started the rug, the Islamic department was being completely renovated and a whole new installation was underway, so I couldn't see any of the rugs. Finally, in October of 1975, I saw the actual rug, one of a pair, and was surprised to see that the colors were more pastel and quite different from mine. If you are interested in this rug and have the opportunity, do visit the "Met" in New York City and see the original.

To make this rug as charted you would have to do the center on 60″ canvas, do the side borders separately, and seam them to the center. When seaming two pieces together, leave off one row on one of the pieces to be worked after they are joined. You would need 6⅔ yards of canvas from the same roll. Use three strands of Persian yarn. (See also page 40.)

I couldn't fit the full width of the rug in my foyer. The area that I will have it in is only 52″ wide, so I used only part of the center and left off the outer borders. My rug measures 108″ long, because the canvas was not quite 10 mesh lengthwise.

When I started stitching, I measured to find the center of my canvas and worked from the center to one end; the other half was rolled up and pinned. When the first half was finished, I worked from the center to the other end. For a while the canvas and I had quite a battle. It hit me in the face more than once, but I soon tamed it. As large as it was, I carried it with me to the hairdresser and so forth until it was about half done, then I kept it on a card table in front of my swivel rocker. That was during the hot summer, and we have no air conditioning. I just peeled down to shorts and a tank top and stitched six to twelve hours a day.

This rug was so much fun to do that I never got tired of it. In fact, I missed it when it was done. It took me eight months to complete.

It takes about 2½ ounces of background yarn for each of the large compartments and about 1 ounce for the smaller ones. The entire rug takes approximately 13 pounds of yarn.

I found it easier to do the outlining of each of the areas before filling in the large areas of color between the outlines.

Be sure to pay attention to the varied spacing in the borders.

A runner could be made by using the width of the large center part, which is 24½" across, and adding the borders to it, which would be another 12", making it 36½" wide.

Rather than using sixteen different symbols to indicate the colors, I used only four and wrote in the color numbers for the rest. I felt that this would be less confusing. It would be useful to color in the areas with colored pencils or to tape a piece of the yarn to the chart.

The colors used were 040 whitish yellow, Y68 light lemon yellow, 442 medium yellow, 441 bright yellow, 426 red orange, 427 burnt orange, 433 dark gold, 445 medium gold, 455 light gold, 395 light blue, 352 blue green, 174 medium brown, 306 dark navy, 166 light gray, 127 lavender gray, and 527 green.

Dotted lines on graphs indicate pattern overlap.

The rug is graphed as follows:

Pages 108–111   Center sections
Pages 112–115   Next lower sections
Pages 116–119   Lower edge and corner

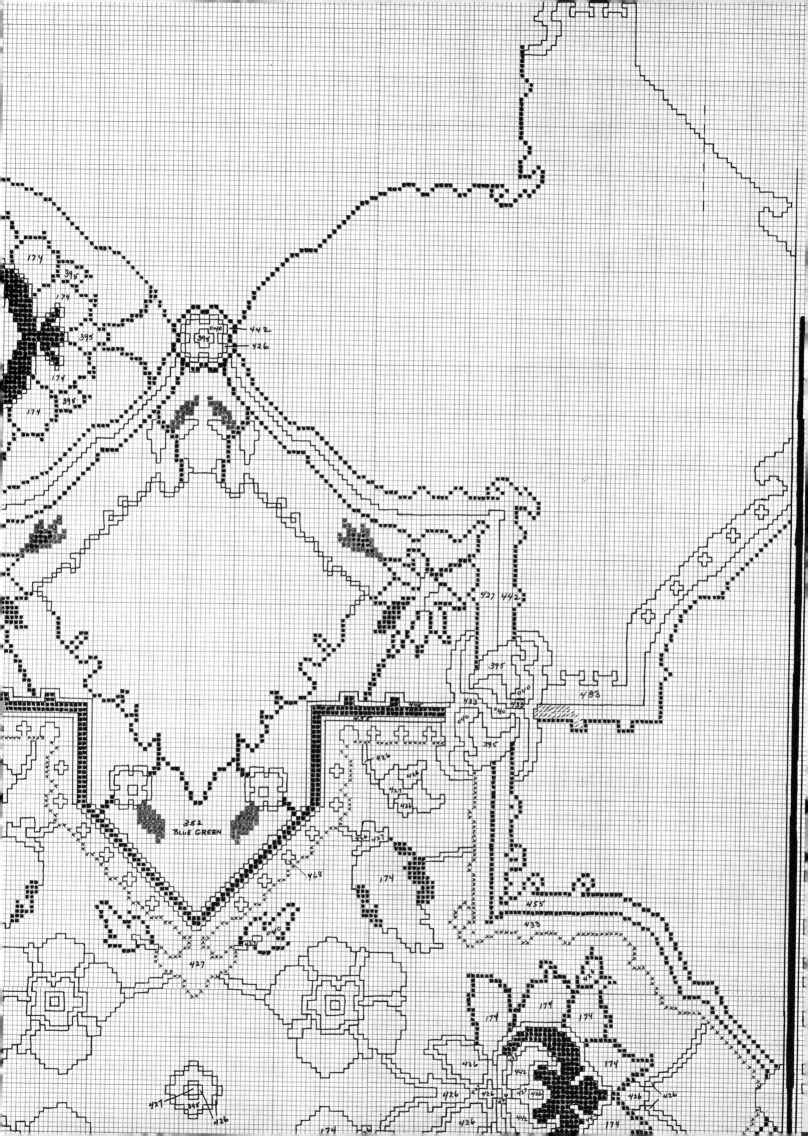

Y68
LIGHT LEMON YELLOW

174
BROWN

Red and Gold Swasti

37⅓″ by 43⅓″ on 10-mesh canvas
31″ by 36″ on 12-mesh canvas

Swasti is a Sanskrit word meaning "happiness" or "fertility." It existed in all eastern cultures of an early date, mainly India, China, and the Caucasus.

The rug shown on plate 22 was worked on 12-mesh canvas with Nantucket Needlework yarn, using the four strands as it comes. The four small squares show other colors. (See plate 23.) The pale aqua on light coral has a row of darker aqua to give a shaded effect. The larger squares (plate 24) have a sculptured look. By doing the pattern in long-arm cross stitch it becomes raised next to the tent stitch ground. The long-arm cross stitch was worked back and forth for three rows on the horizontal lines and three stitches wide on the vertical lines. On 10-mesh canvas a full square measures 6½″. Each square added to it would be another 6″. Use three strands of Persian yarn on 10-mesh canvas for the long-arm cross stitch, and all three strands for the tent stitch.

To enlarge this design, just add as many blocks of the pattern as needed. Each additional block on 10-mesh adds 3″.

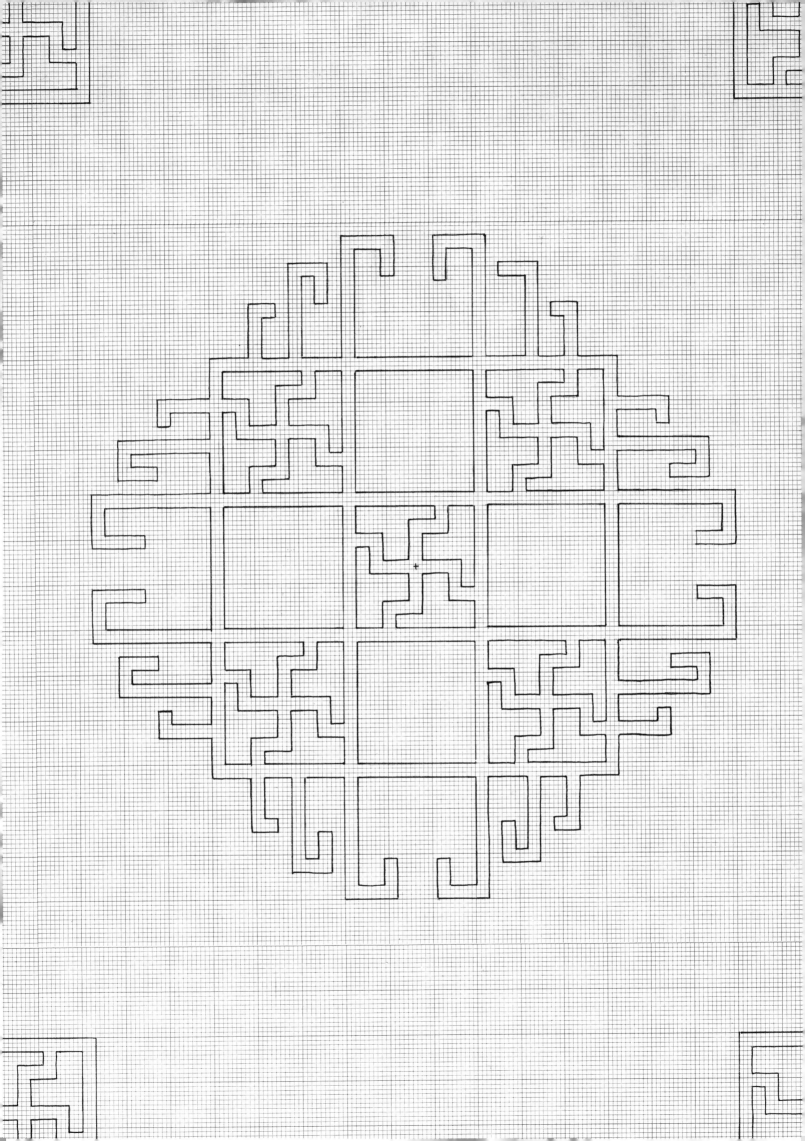

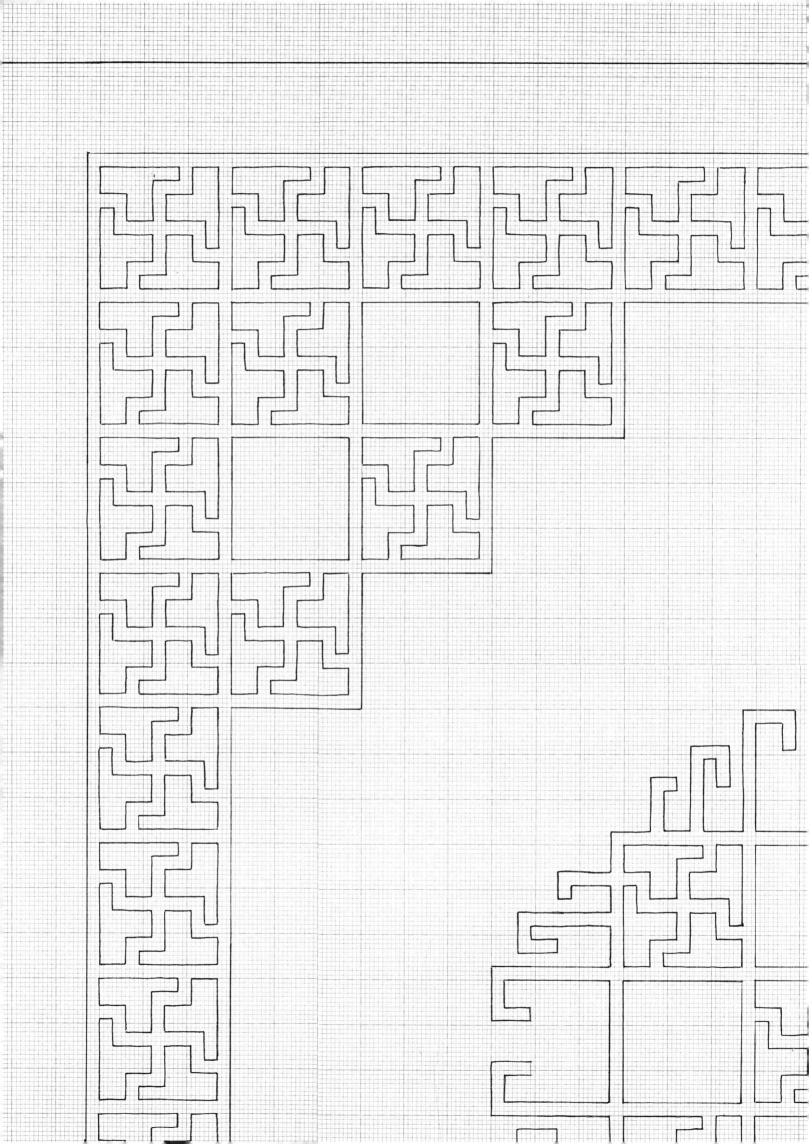

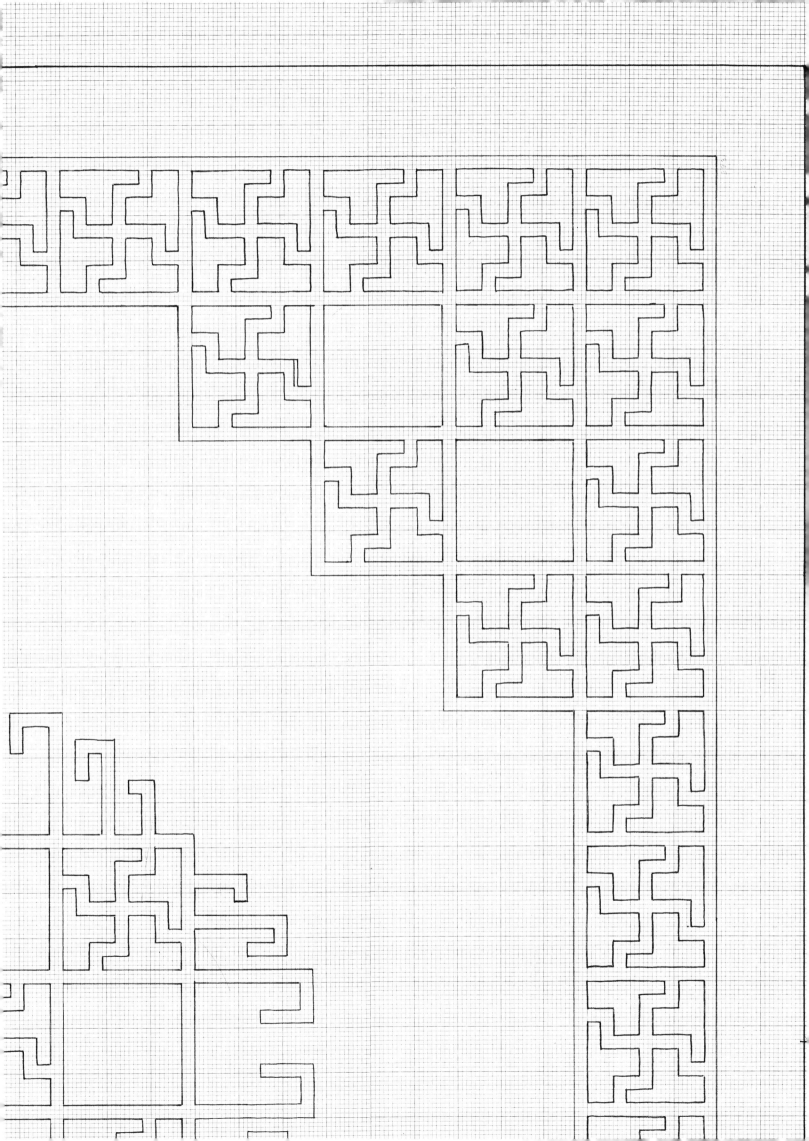

Blue-Green Bargello Rug
with Tent Stitch Border

37½" by 50½" on 12-mesh canvas
each motif measures 10" by 11"

This was worked on 12-mesh canvas with three strands of Persian yarn for the bargello and two strands for the tent stitch. (See plate 25.)

The light blue background between the motifs could be worked in tent stitch, which would be very effective.

I did a row of long-arm cross stitch around the outer edge, which gives the appearance of a braid. Use two strands of yarn.

You need 1⅔ yards of 40" 12-mesh canvas. I used approximately ¼ pound each of 012 off-white, 532 medium green, and 530 dark green; ½ pound each of 396 light blue and 352 blue green.

To make a rug 45" by 62" you would use 10-mesh canvas. Two yards of 60" width would be required. You would then use four or five strands of yarn for bargello and three strands for tent stitch. On the 60" width you could also add one more motif in width and of course as many in length as you want, provided you have the length of canvas needed. Each motif measures 12" wide and 13¼" long on the 10-mesh canvas, that is, if the canvas is 10 mesh in both directions.

It's best to measure carefully or count to find the exact center of the pattern, marked with a + on the chart, then work the center motif and the motifs on each side of the center. Roll up one end of the canvas to where you are working and pin it. Continue working on half of the bargello. By the time you have finished this half, the canvas should be limp enough so that when you unroll the second half to work, the first half won't fight you.

When the center is completed, do the border motifs along a short edge to each corner. There will be three rows of medium green and eight rows of blue green between the center bargello and the border bargello motifs.

NOTE: On the long side edges, the chart appears to have only two rows of the medium green. There are *three* rows. The first row is worked on the first thread and partly tucks under the bargello stitch.

The spacing between the border motifs is different on the long sides from on the short sides.

To make a little finer stitch, this rug could be worked on 13-mesh canvas, which would measure about 29″ by 35″. My 12-mesh canvas was 12½ mesh in length and 12 mesh in width. On the 13-mesh each motif should measure 8¾″ wide and 9¼″ long.

If you enlarge the rug by adding additional motifs you may have to adjust the spacing of the border motifs.

Dotted lines on graphs indicate pattern overlap.

The Junior League of New York did this rug in shades of coral for an auction. (See plate 26.)

By enlarging one of the motifs, I made a 13″ pillow in a yellow-gold coloring. (See plate 27.)

The three-color combinations would be as follows:

Blue Green	Coral	Yellow
PATERNA PERSIAN		BUCILLA
012 off-white	005 white	1 white
396 light blue	492 golden beige	135 lemon frost
352 blue green	425 flesh	2 light yellow
532 medium green	852 medium coral	3 dark yellow
530 dark green	843 dark coral	153 tobacco gold

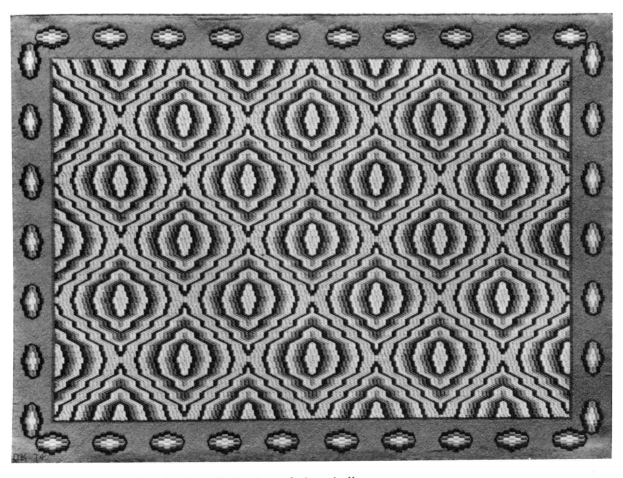

The rug is shown here horizontally but is graphed vertically.

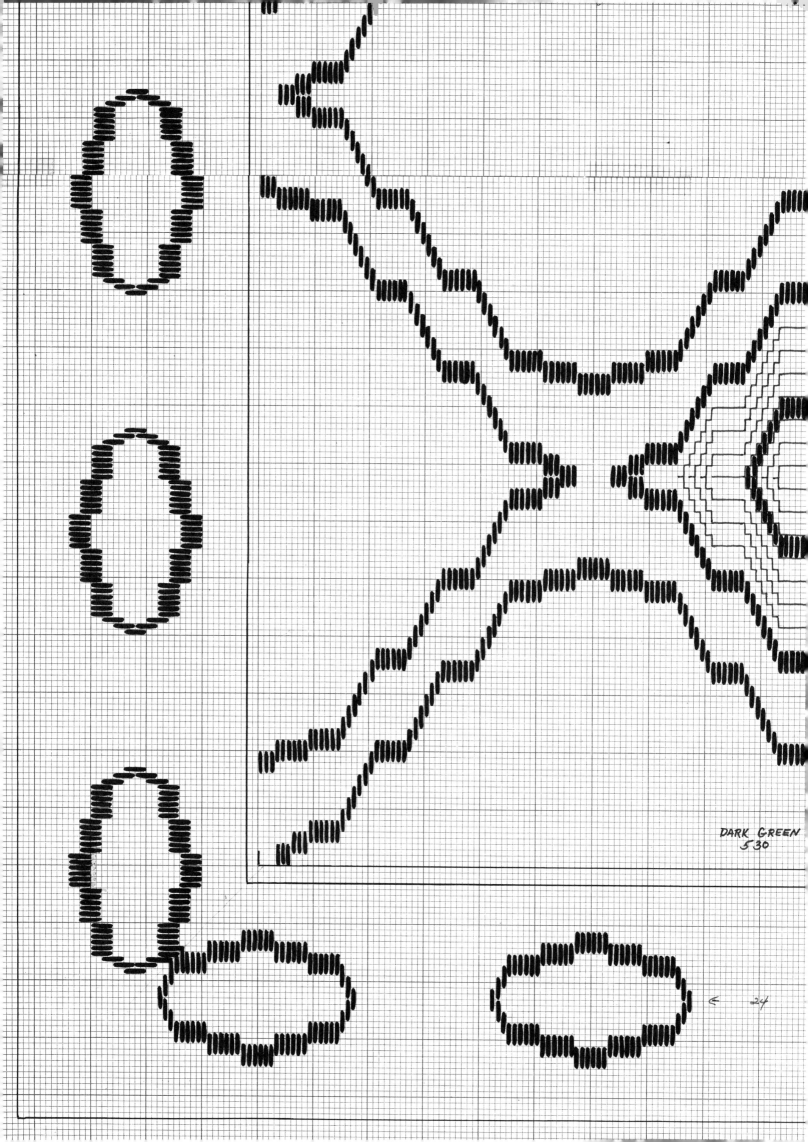

DARK GREEN
530

E 24

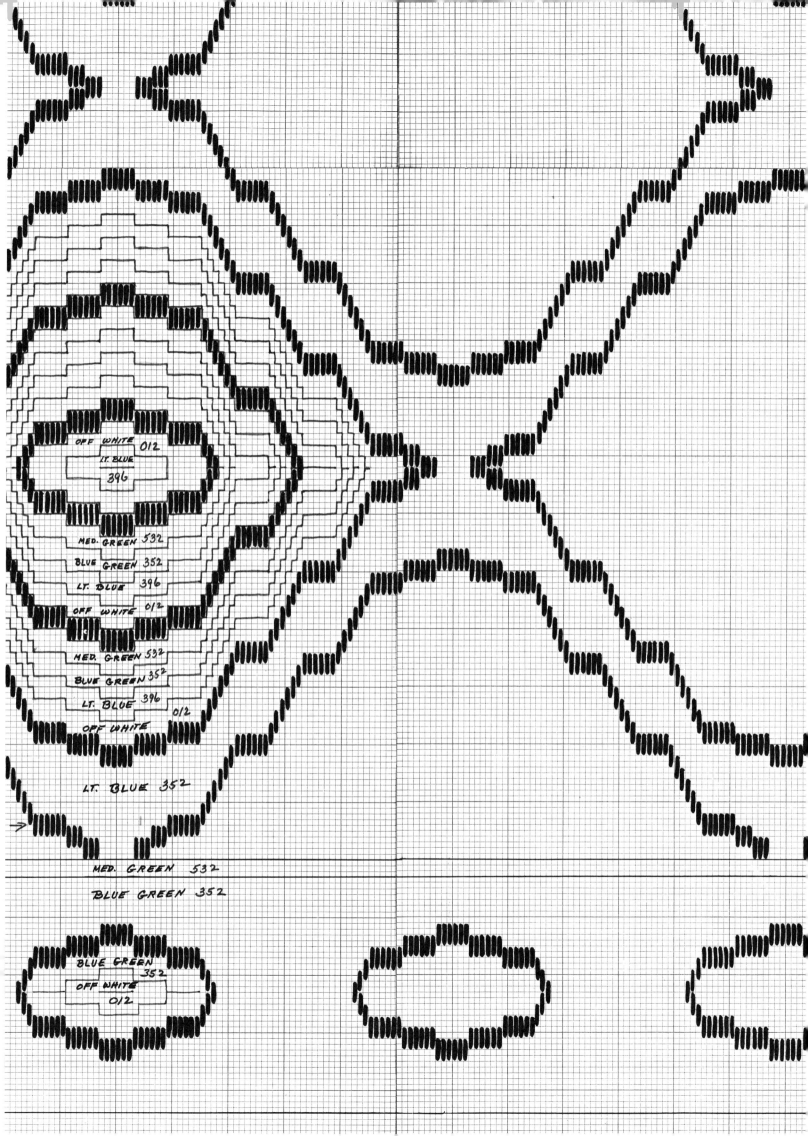

OFF WHITE 012
LT. BLUE
396
MED. GREEN 532
BLUE GREEN 352
LT. BLUE 396
OFF WHITE 012
MED. GREEN 532
BLUE GREEN 352
LT. BLUE 396
OFF WHITE 012
LT. BLUE 352
MED. GREEN 532
BLUE GREEN 352
BLUE GREEN 352
OFF WHITE 012

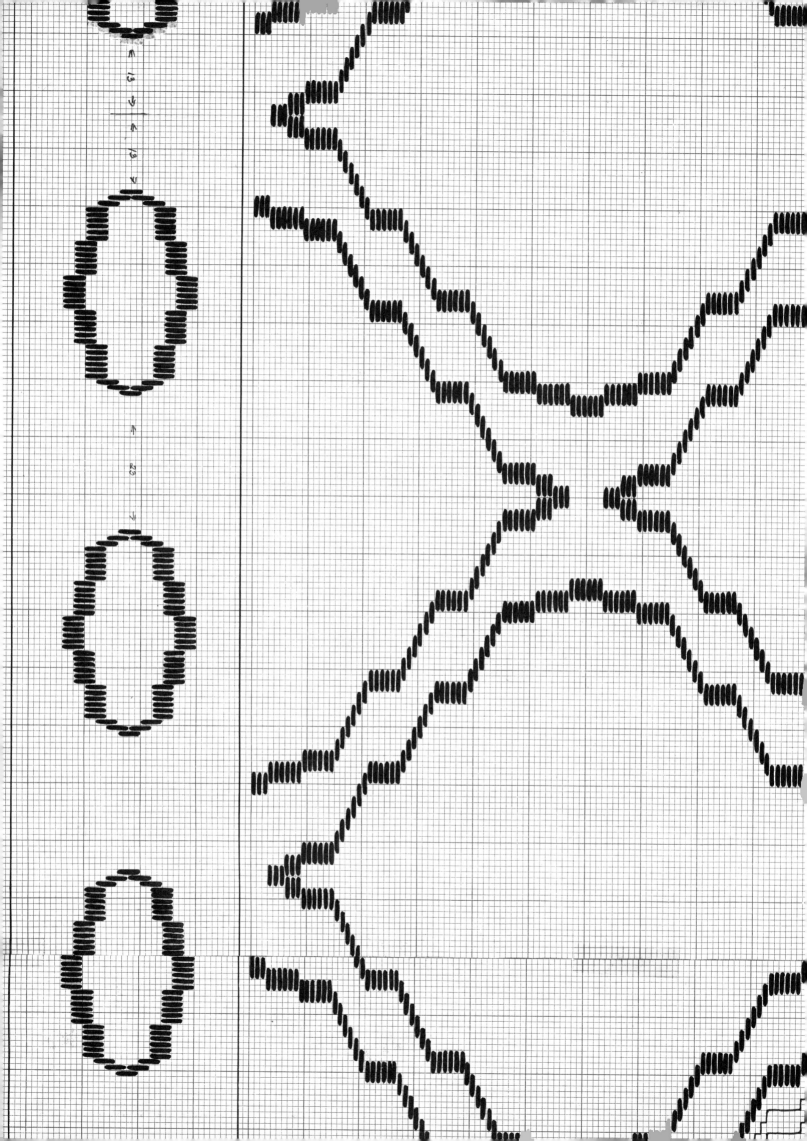

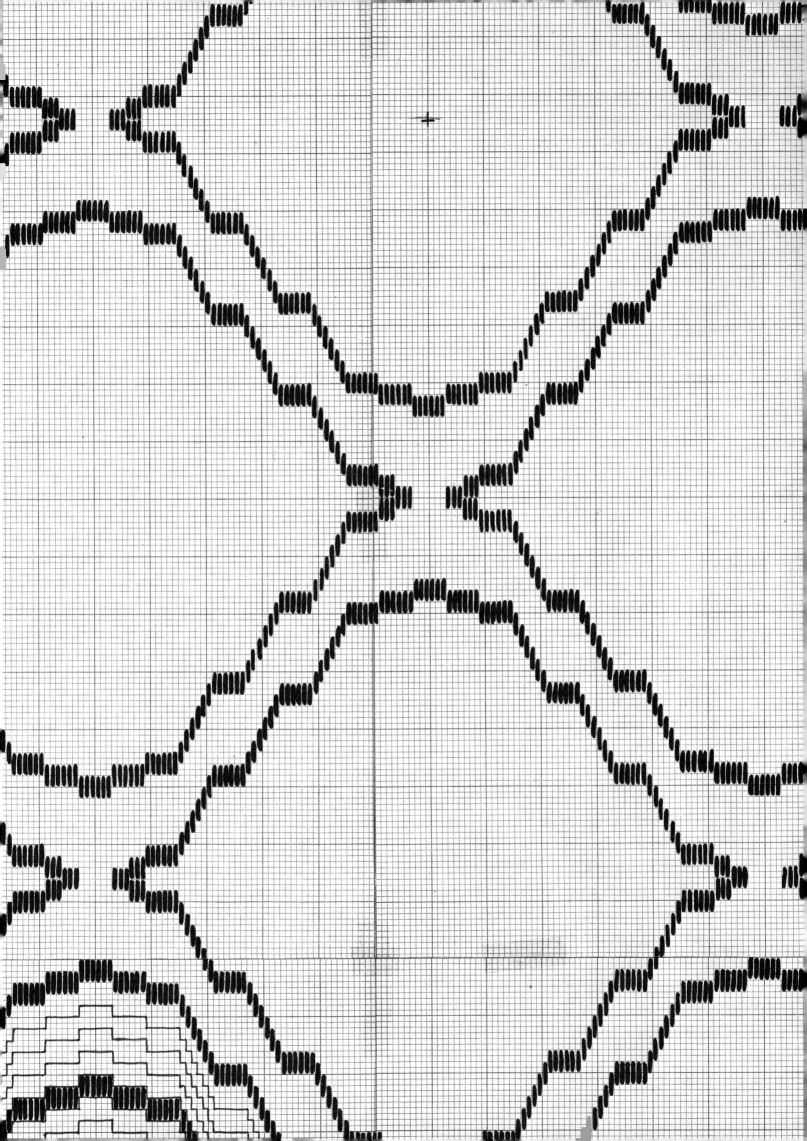

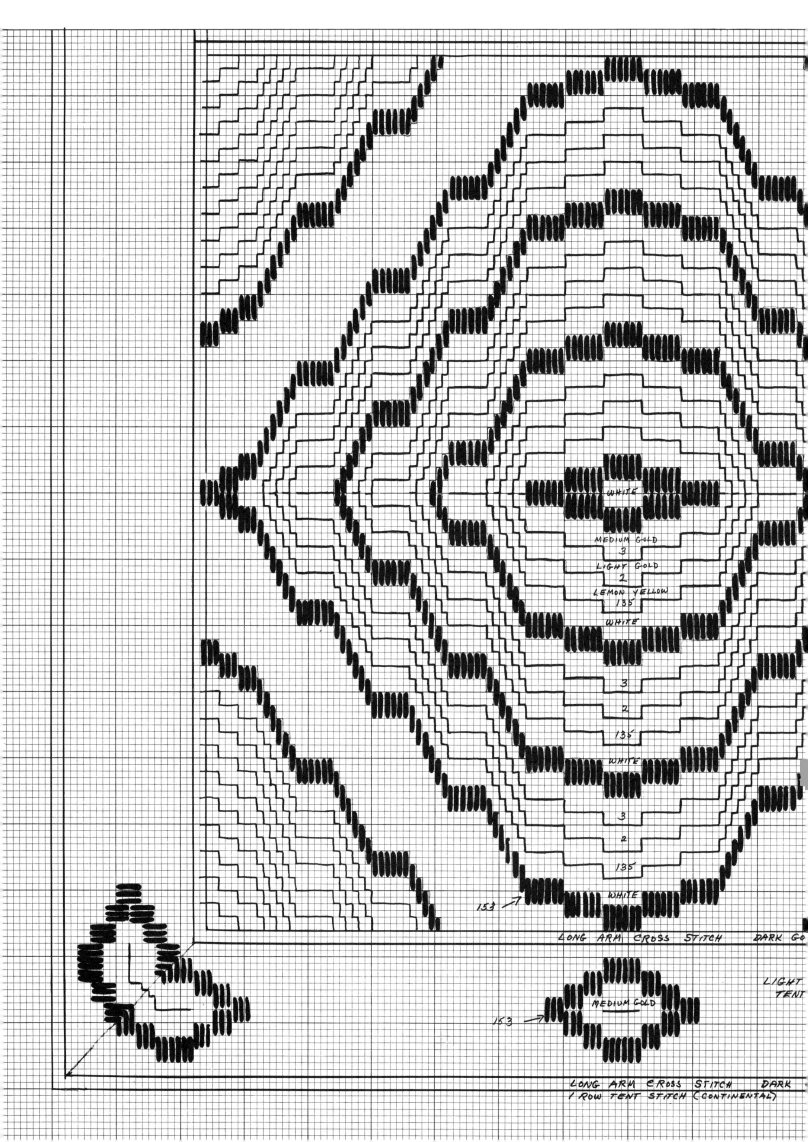

WHITE

MEDIUM GOLD
3
LIGHT GOLD
2
LEMON YELLOW
135
WHITE

3

2

135

WHITE

3

2

135

WHITE

153 ↗

LONG ARM CROSS STITCH   DARK GO

LIGHT
TENT

MEDIUM GOLD

153 ↗

LONG ARM CROSS STITCH   DARK
1 ROW TENT STITCH (CONTINENTAL)

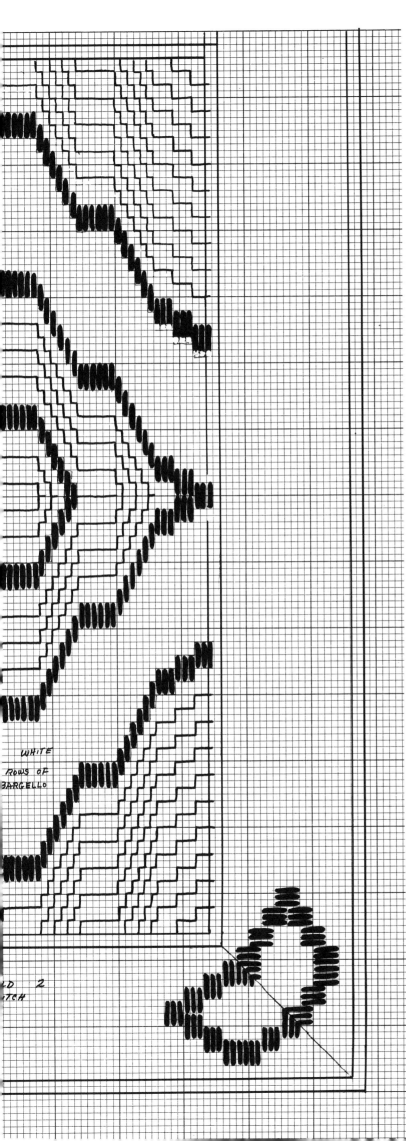

WHITE
ROWS OF
BARGELLO

LD   2
ITCH

Yellow-Gold Bargello Pillow

Stair Risers and Treads

In my first book, *Four Way Bargello*, there was a picture of my stair risers. It was just shown in a miscellaneous chapter and no patterns were included. I had a number of inquiries about them, so here are the drawings.

Each stair was done separately, so if any accident should occur one can be taken off and repaired. I used No. 5 penelope canvas, 40″ wide. The worked area measures 19″ by 38″, which includes the riser and the tread.

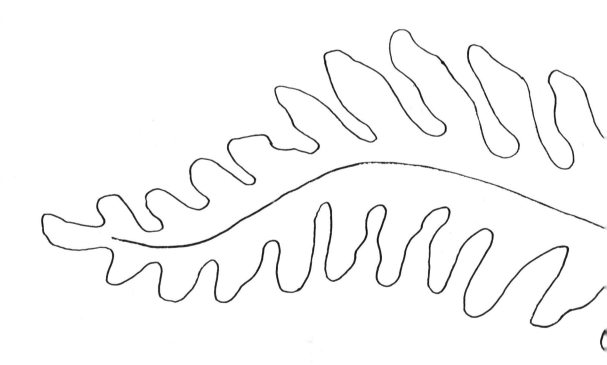

The design is worked in every hole, ten stitches to an inch, while the background was worked in the large holes only, five stitches to an inch. For the design, use three strands of Persian yarn, but for the background, use nine strands.

The fern on each side goes partway on the tread. When tracing it on your canvas have the lowest leaf about six stitches or a little more than 1″ from the edge of the working area. The fern should be enlarged to 15½″ long. The drawing shows the fern for one side only; flip it over for the other side. The center drawings should be about 8″ high at the most.

Since our house is a split-level, I needed only seven risers; if you have a full flight of stairs you will need more. You could alternate a riser with full design and one with the ferns only.

Use colorplate 28 as a guide for your shading.

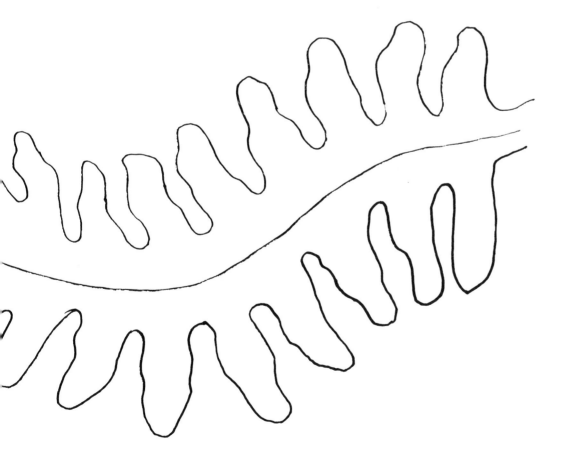

149

Dragon

38½" by 55"

Miss Polly Trees brought me a lovely light blue linen tablecloth embroidered in white so that I could copy the design. Her mother bought this in China many years ago when she was living there. The design was of five dragons thrashing in and out of the clouds or ocean. They were spitting flaming pearls at one another. Polly suggested that I use the design for a rug, which I did, rearranging the design a bit to elongate it.

The rug shown here is the center dragon of Polly's rug. Mrs. F. Douglas Adams, Jr., of Darien stitched this one.

Instead of charting the dragon, I have made a drawing, but did chart the border for accuracy. It should be quite easy to follow the coloring in plate 29. The best way to do the scales is to stitch each outline in the lightest shade, then follow inside this with two succeeding darker shades.

Since this is a combination of a chart and a drawing, it might be advisable to do the charted borders first; then you will know how much to enlarge the drawing so that it will fit within the borders. If you use 10-mesh canvas (which the original was worked on) the drawing should be enlarged to fit within an area of 27" x 44".

After tracing the drawing onto your canvas, see General Working Instructions at the beginning of this book and draw in your border, being careful to center the interior part. Instead of drawing in the border, you could count it from the chart as you stitch.

I have not given any color numbers, because this design can be done in various combinations. Use three strands of Persian yarn on 10-mesh canvas.

Center

Center

Three Giraffes

38″ by 64″ on 10-mesh canvas

Mrs. L. J. Schettino did this rug. It was a painted design, but I have made a chart for it. (See plate 30.)

This chart was done in two sections with a duplicate piece of the design so that they can be fitted together. Arrows point to a few stitches in each section that overlap. Each section is really a design in itself and would make good hangings or smaller rugs.

On 10-mesh canvas use three strands of Persian yarn.

Some of the spots have been shaded in on the chart; shade the remainder accordingly. You can refer to the colorplate. The color numbers are written on the chart. They are 382 blue and 593 for the background; white and black for the eyes; 492, 466, 420, 410, 154, and 172 browns for the giraffes; 134 taupe and 131 gold brown for the tree trunks; 574, G54, G64, 505, 555, 553, 590, 542, 520, and 504 for the leaves.

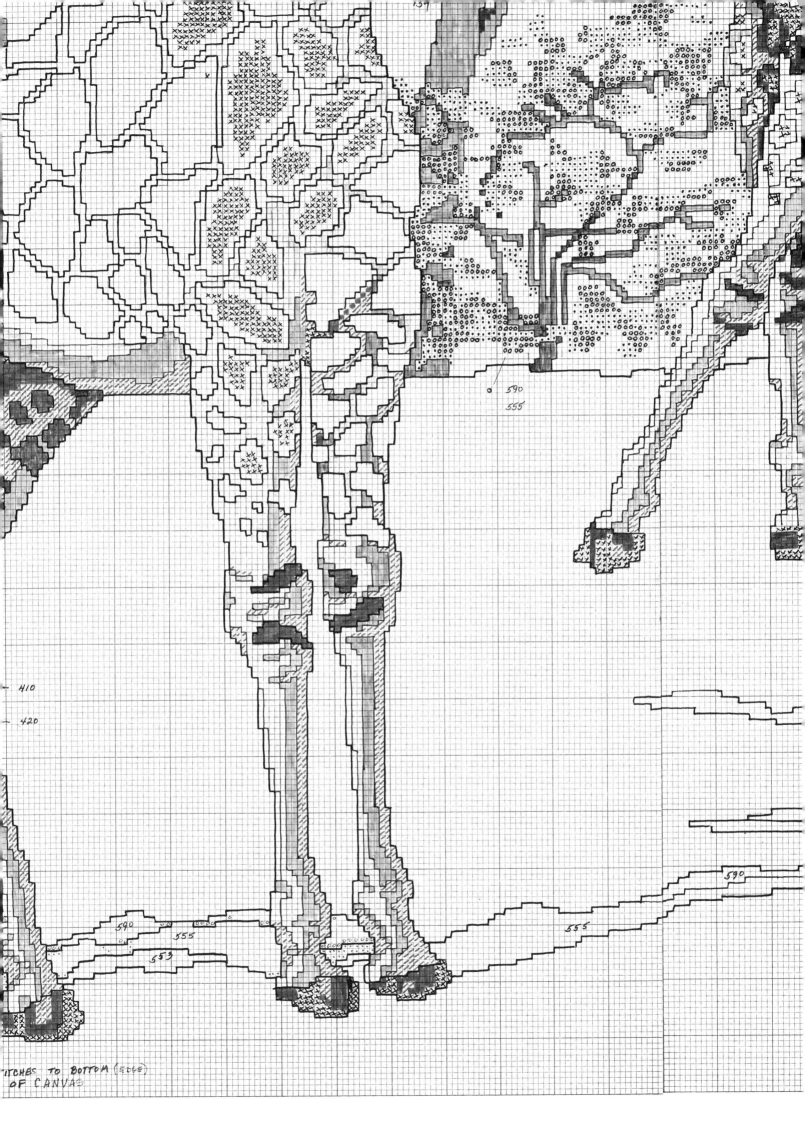

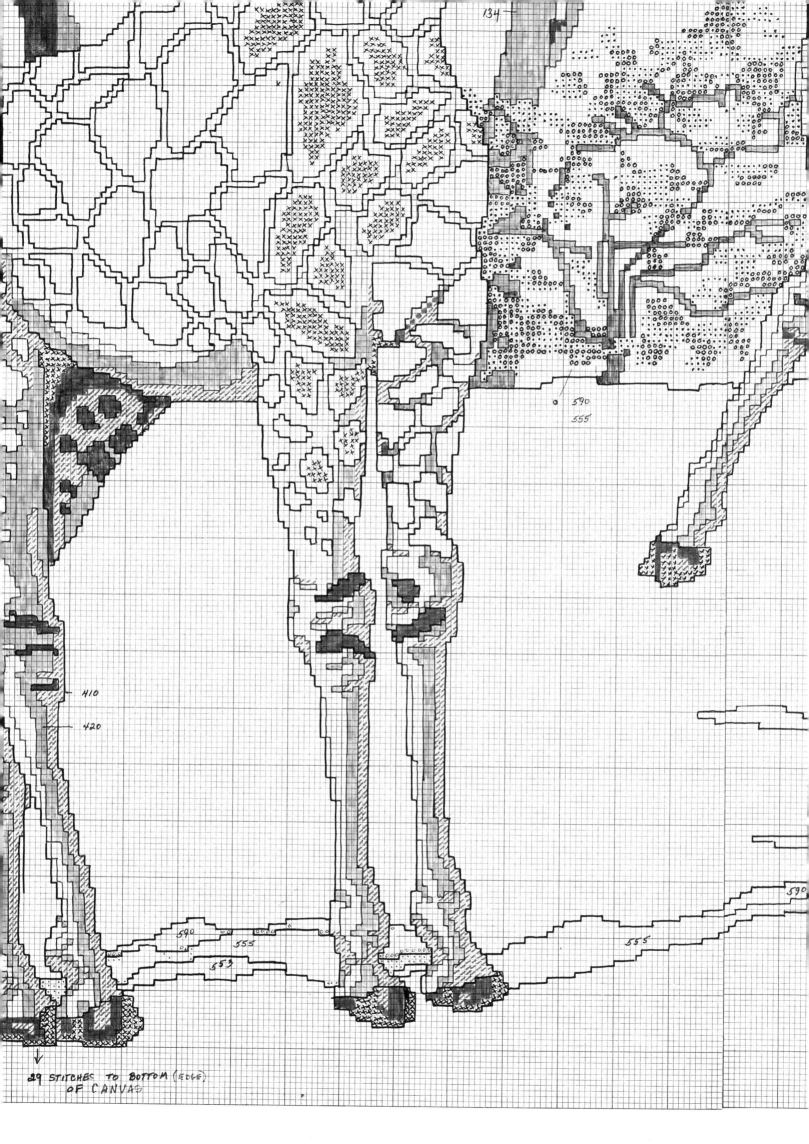

134

590
555

410

420

590

590
555
555
653

29 STITCHES TO BOTTOM (EDGE)
OF CANVAS

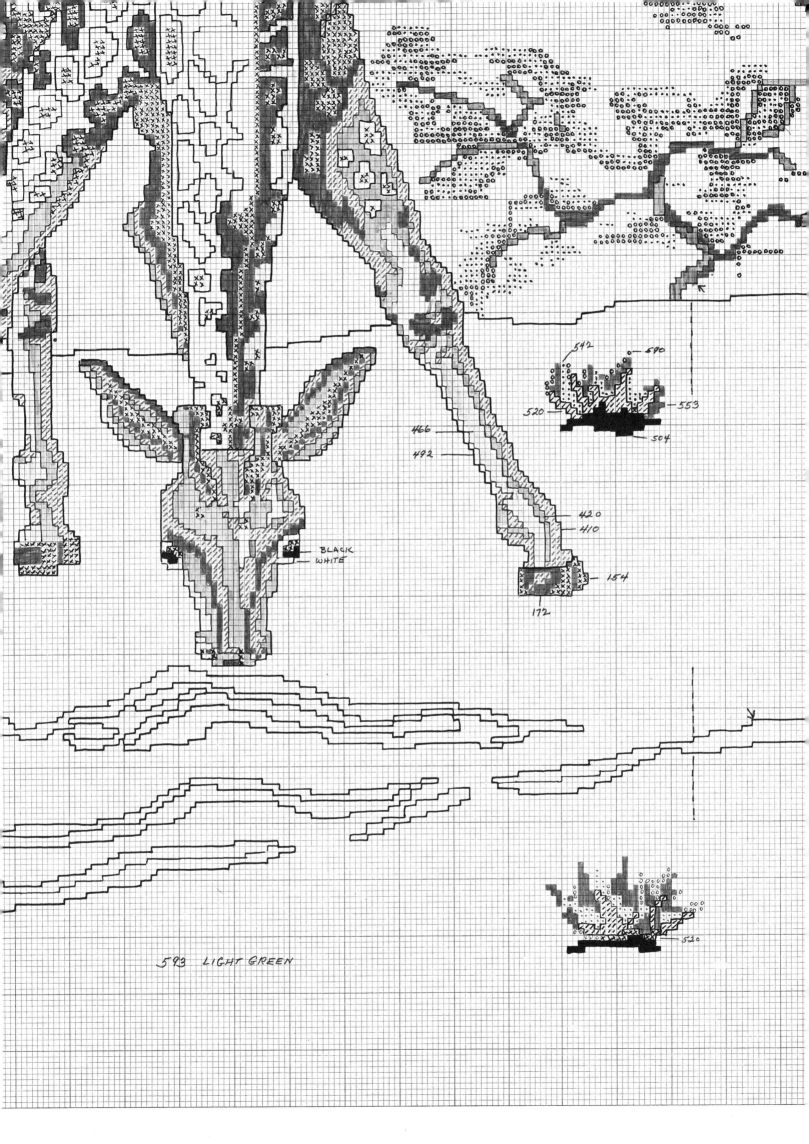

542
590
520
553
504

466
492

420
410

BLACK
WHITE

154

172

593 LIGHT GREEN

520

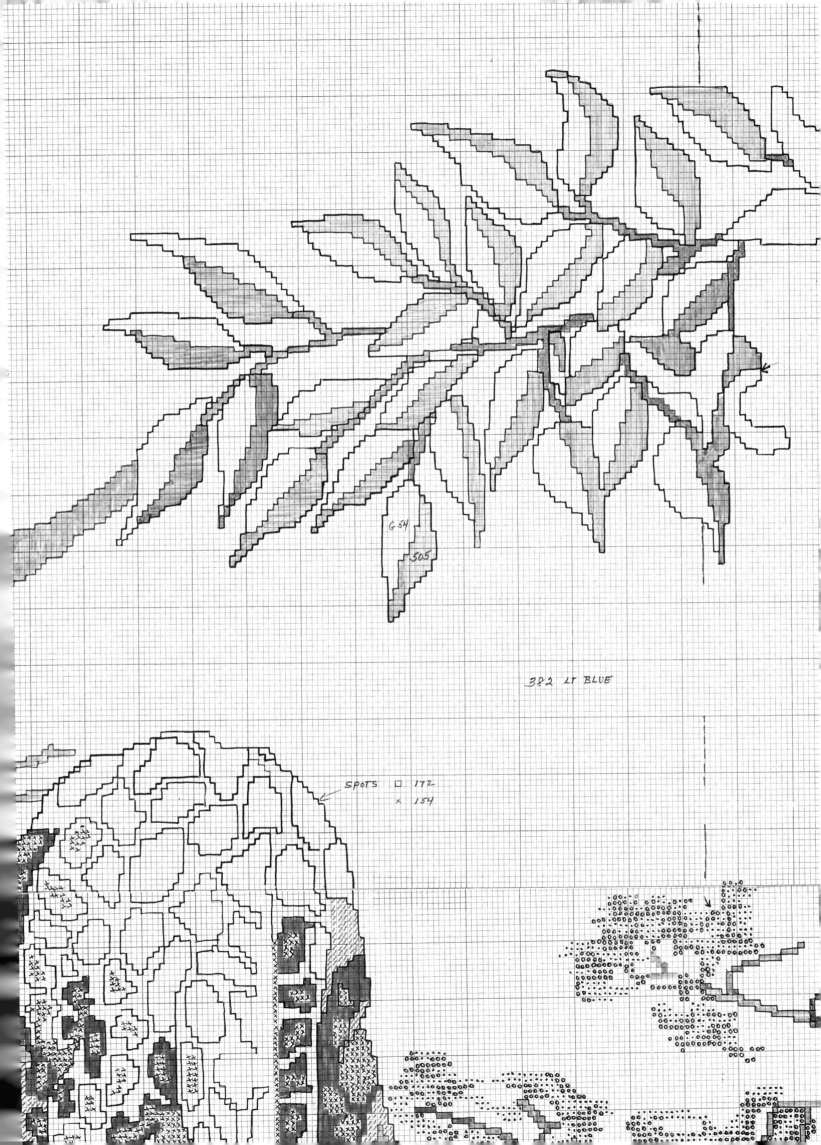

G 54

505

382 LT BLUE

SPOTS □ 172
× 154

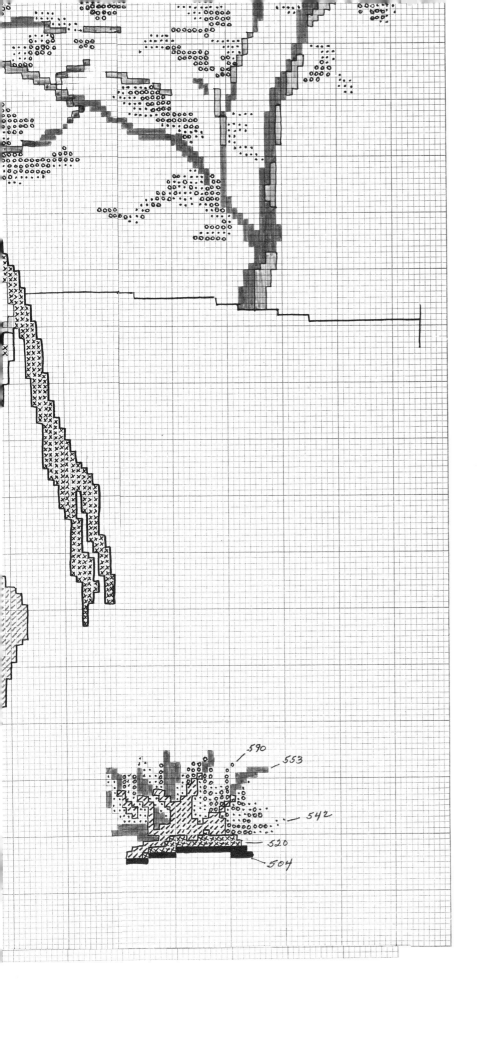

590

553

542

520

504

168

Odds and Ends

Any avid needleworker has scads of leftover yarn. Here is a small rug made with some of my leftovers. (See plate 31.)

I used the long-arm cross stitch on 10-mesh canvas and three strands of Persian yarn. There was some thought given to the use of color. I separated the colors I wanted to use from the other colors in my big bag of yarn. See plate 31. For the border, I used off-whites and very pale shades.

This rug reminds me of the old "hit-or-miss" rugs that were hooked or woven years ago.

The size of the rug can vary according to the quantity of yarn that you have. If you want a larger rug perhaps you can beg some of your friends' leftovers that they don't intend to use and are about to throw out.

The center part of the rug was worked back and forth, working across and turning the canvas to work back again. The borders were worked around in one direction, giving a frame effect. You could work one large framed piece or several framed blocks in the one rug.

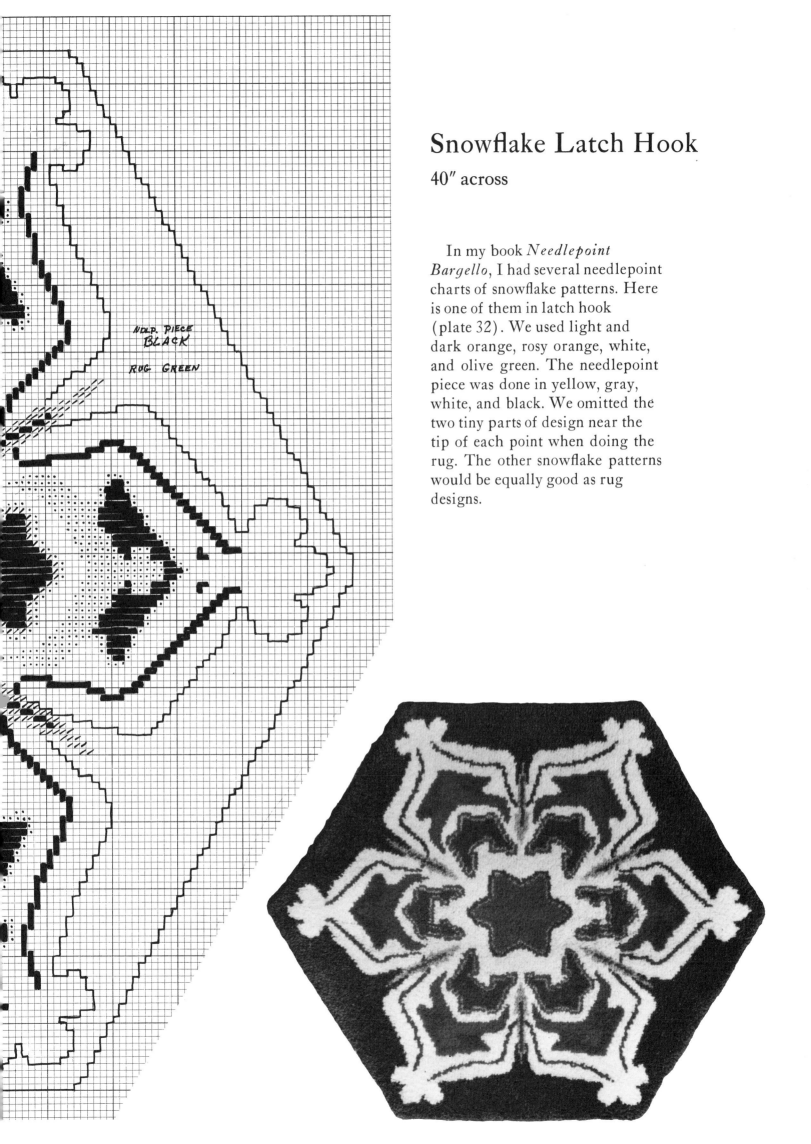

Snowflake Latch Hook

40″ across

In my book *Needlepoint Bargello*, I had several needlepoint charts of snowflake patterns. Here is one of them in latch hook (plate 32). We used light and dark orange, rosy orange, white, and olive green. The needlepoint piece was done in yellow, gray, white, and black. We omitted the two tiny parts of design near the tip of each point when doing the rug. The other snowflake patterns would be equally good as rug designs.

NDLP. PIECE
BLACK

RUG GREEN

Doll-House Rugs

There is so much interest in doll houses that I have included several rugs for them. The first one is described on page 31 with the Iranian multiblock rug (plates 7 and 8). All these were worked on 18-mesh canvas with one strand of Persian yarn.

Red and Gold Persian
3¾″ by 5¾″

The colors used were 334 dark blue, 385 medium blue, 445 gold, 015 pale gold, and R50 red. I cut away the excess canvas, leaving ½″ at the ends, then pulled out the cross threads of canvas to make a fringe (plate 33).

334 R50 445 385

015

TOP

66

174